INTERNATIONAL PERSI
ON TRANSITION TO SCHOOL

With increasing attention given by governments and policy makers to children's transition to school, and the associated need for educators, families and communities to be supported in the process, changes are often required to existing structures and pedagogy.

This book is framed around the notion of transition as a time of change for those involved in the transition process and as a time for reconceptualising beliefs, policy and practice.

It explores transition from a number of international perspectives and raises issues around the coherence of:

- how children perceive and respond to starting school;
- the roles and expectations of parents;
- developmental changes for parents;
- supporting children with diverse learning needs;
- how policy, curriculum and pedagogy are conceived and implemented.

Readers will be informed about current practices and issues arising out of research in Europe, Scandinavia, the United Kingdom and Australia and will be stimulated to consider how they can change their own transition beliefs, policies and practices.

International Perspectives on Transition to School is essential reading for researchers and educators and anyone wanting to know more about the transition to school and how to support young children, their families and schools.

Kay Margetts is Associate Professor in Early Childhood Studies, and Director of International Baccalaureate Programs in the Melbourne Graduate School of Education at the University of Melbourne, Australia.

Anna Kienig is Assistant Professor in Developmental Psychology, Deputy Dean for Student Affairs and Coordinator of International Programs (Socrates/Erasmus) at the University of Bialystock, Poland.

INTERNATIONAL PERSPECTIVES ON TRANSITION TO SCHOOL

Reconceptualising beliefs, policy and practice

Edited by Kay Margetts and Anna Kienig

Routledge
Taylor & Francis Group

LONDON AND NEW YORK

First published 2013
by Routledge
2 Park Square, Milton Park, Abingdon, Oxon OX14 4RN

Simultaneously published in the USA and Canada
by Routledge
711 Third Avenue, New York, NY 10017

Routledge is an imprint of the Taylor & Francis Group, an informa business

British Library Cataloguing in Publication Data
A catalogue record for this book is available from the British Library

Library of Congress Cataloging in Publication Data
International perspectives on transition to school : reconceptualising beliefs, policy and practice / edited by Kay Margetts and Anna Kienig.
pages cm
Includes bibliographical references.
ISBN 978-0-415-53612-7 (hardback) -- ISBN 978-0-415-53613-4 (pbk.) -- ISBN 978-0-203-11180-2 (ebook) 1. Readiness for school. 2. Education, Elementary. I. Margetts, Kay, editor of compilation. II. Kienig, Anna, editor of compilation.
LB1132.I58 2013
372.21--dc23
2012047050

ISBN: 978-0-415-53612-7 (hbk)
ISBN: 978-0-415-53613-4 (pbk)
ISBN: 978-0-203-11180-2 (ebk)

Typeset in Bembo
by Saxon Graphics Ltd, Derby

MIX
Paper from
responsible sources
FSC
www.fsc.org   FSC® C013056

Printed and bound in Great Britain by
TJ International Ltd, Padstow, Cornwall

CONTENTS

LIST OF FIGURES AND TABLES

Figures

Tables

CONTRIBUTORS

Stig Broström is Professor in Early Childhood Education at Aarhus University, Department of Education (DPU), Denmark. His main areas of research are related to educational and curriculum theories, children's life in preschool day care and the first years in school with focus on children's play, social competence and friendship. Currently, he is engaged in a research programme focusing on day care professionals' view on children's learning and early literacy. He is head of the Childhood, Learning and Curriculum Theory Research Unit.

Sue Dockett is Professor in Early Childhood Education, Charles Sturt University, New South Wales, Australia. Sue has been involved in early childhood teacher education and research since 1988. Much of her research is focused on educational transitions, particularly transitions to school and the expectations, experiences and perceptions of all involved, and with Bob Perry, she has published widely both nationally and internationally in these areas. Integral to the investigations of educational transitions is a commitment to incorporating children's perspectives. Together with Bob Perry, Sue was instrumental in the development of the recent *Transition to School: Position Statement* by a group of international researchers (Educational Transitions and Change (ETC) Research Group 2011).

Aline-Wendy Dunlop is Emeritus Professor in the School of Education, Faculty of Humanities and Social Sciences, University of Strathclyde, Glasgow and also an independent author and researcher. She has researched transitions policy and practices and her longitudinal study focuses on a group of children as they navigate the school system from pre-school through primary and secondary education into adult life. She is on the executive of the Scottish Educational

Research Association, a Vice-President of Early Education and country coordinator for EECERA.

Johanna Einarsdottir is Professor of Early Childhood Education at the School of Education, University of Iceland. She has been involved in early childhood education and early childhood teacher education for around 40 years. She is currently the director of the Center for Research in Early Childhood Education at the University of Iceland. Johanna's professional interests focus on children's views about their preschool and school experiences associated with commencing school. Johanna has published widely.

Hilary Fabian has many years of experience as a teacher of young children in London, Buckinghamshire, Shropshire and with the Service Children's Education Authority in Germany. She commenced work in the university sector in 1991: first at Manchester Metropolitan University where she was course leader for the Early Years Continuing Professional Development programmes; then at the University of Edinburgh; and then as Leader of Education and Childhood Studies at North East Wales Institute/Glyndwr University. Hilary's publications and consultancies reflect her interest in educational transitions, particularly children starting school, children transferring between schools and the manner in which the induction of children and families to new settings is managed.

Wilfried Griebel, Dipl.-Psych., has been working since 1982 as a member of the scientific staff at the State Institute for Early Childhood Education and Research (IFP) in Munich, Bavaria, Germany. His research initially focused on fathers in different family structures and family transitions for post-divorce families and stepfamilies. In the field of early childhood education, together with Renate Niesel, he has undertaken considerable work on interactions between family and educational institutions, especially the transition from family to kindergarten and from kindergarten to school. His current work on transition to school focuses on the developmental transitions of families during this time.

Elizabeth F. S. Hannah is a senior lecturer in educational psychology at the School of Education, Social Work and Community Education at the University of Dundee, Scotland. She is currently Director for MScEdPsy and MEdPsy Programmes. She has worked as an educational psychologist in a number of local authorities in Scotland since qualifying in the early 1980s and latterly was a deputy principal educational psychologist in East Dunbartonshire Council. Her professional interests as an educational psychologist have included educational transitions, the inclusion of children and young people with additional support needs, promoting children's mental health and well-being, consulting with children and action research.

Ole Henrik Hansen is a PhD fellow in early childhood education at Aarhus University, Department of Education (DPU), Denmark. His field of research is the young child up to 3 years of age, with focus on language, social and cultural inclusion and body competences. His PhD project aims to combine various scientific areas such as biology, curriculum theory, postmodern psychology and phenomenology. He is a member of the Childhood, Learning and Curriculum Theory Research Unit.

Anders Skriver Jensen is a PhD fellow in early childhood education at Aarhus University, Department of Education (DPU), Denmark. He is currently working with early literacy within a sociocultural framework, investigating how early literacy curriculum in day care services and the first years of school might be connected in a unified approach. He is a member of the Childhood, Learning and Curriculum Theory Research Unit.

Divya Jindal-Snape is Professor of Education, Inclusion and Life Transitions at the University of Dundee, Scotland. Her research interests lie in the field of inclusion and educational transitions. A significant proportion of her work has been with children and young people with additional support needs, especially children and young people with visual impairment, autism, learning difficulties and emotional and behavioural needs. Divya is Convenor of the Transformative Change: Educational and Life Transitions (TCELT) research group of the School of Education, Social Work and Community Education. She has acted as research consultant for Communities Scotland, Dundee International Women's Centre, Volunteer Development Scotland, Scottish Centre for Research in Community Learning and Development, University of Surrey and Youth Link.

Anna Kienig is Assistant Professor in Developmental Psychology, Deputy Dean for Student Affairs and Coordinator of International Programs (Socrates/ Erasmus) at the University of Bialystock, Poland. She teaches in a range of subjects including early childhood development, curriculum, learning and teaching and professional practice. Her research has a primary focus on children's transition to school. Anna has co-authored one book and has chapters in five other books. She is also an editor/co-editor of two journals.

Kay Margetts is Associate Professor in Early Childhood Studies, and Director of International Baccalaureate Programs in the Melbourne Graduate School of Education at the University of Melbourne, Australia. She has been involved in early childhood and primary teacher education since 1996 following many years as a preschool teacher in a variety of settings. Her research and publications have focused mostly on children's transition, adjustment and progress in primary school and early years curriculum and pedagogy.

Renate Niesel, Dipl.-Psych., has been a member of the scientific staff at the State Institute of Early Childhood Education and Research (IFP) in Munich, Germany. She started working on transitions in the context of divorce and the adaptations and coping strategies of parents and children. Transferring her experience from family transitions to early childhood education, she carried out empirical studies with Wilfried Griebel on the transition from family to kindergarten and from kindergarten to school in Bavaria, Germany. Prior to her retirement she was involved in work with Wilfried and others on parents' transitions as their children commence school.

Mary O'Kane is undertaking postdoctoral research at the Dublin Institute of Technology in Ireland after completing her PhD in 2007. At the time, Mary's thesis was one of the few pieces of research in Ireland in the area of transition to school.

Bob Perry is Professor of Education, School of Education, Charles Sturt University, Albury, Australia. He is primarily involved in the development of the research ethos in the Faculty of Education and nurturing early career researchers. His main areas of research include early childhood mathematics education and, with Sue Dockett; educational transitions and the education of indigenous students. Together with Sue Dockett, Bob was instrumental in the development of the aspirational *Transition to School: Position Statement* (Educational Transitions and Change (ETC) Research Group 2011).

Anne Petriwskyj is Adjunct Associate Professor in the School of Early Childhood, Queensland University of Technology, Brisbane, Australia. She has a professional background working with children with diverse abilities and cultural backgrounds and with their families, teachers and communities, mainly in rural and remote areas of Australia. This work has included childcare, preschool, kindergarten, the early years of school, gifted and disability education, programmes for children who speak languages other than English and indigenous children. Her research on transition to school focuses on the ways transition processes can become more inclusive, so as to support the educational participation rights of all children.

ACKNOWLEDGEMENTS

The editors, Kay Margetts and Anna Kienig, acknowledge the authors in this book who have contributed significantly to the development of debate, research and discussion around transition to primary school. Each one has contributed to the reconceptualising of transition to school and associated changes that have occurred in educational policy and practice that will hopefully continue to evolve.

PART I
Introduction

1

A CONCEPTUAL FRAMEWORK FOR TRANSITION

Kay Margetts and Anna Kienig

Introduction

Associated with an increasing focus across the world on the development and provision of universal high quality early childhood education and care for children from birth, many governments are also establishing policies to support children's transition into formal schooling. These trends recognise the importance of early experiences for children's ongoing learning, development and success at both the personal level and the national level, and are frequently associated with the reconceptualisation of beliefs, policy, traditions and practice. In some countries this has included significant changes to the school system itself, including changes to the starting school age. It is important that all those involved and impacted by ensuing changes – policy makers, as well as staff in schools and early childhood services, children and families, allied professionals and communities – are supported and given voice in the processes.

Transitions and the associated processes of change or movement from one situation or activity to another have long been conceived as part of the passage of life, and the associated adaptations as a lifelong, continuous process (Elder 1998), as a 'rite of passage' (van Gennep 1960), as a 'border-crossing' (Campbell Clark 2000) and as 'rites of institution' (Bourdieu 1997 cited in Webb, Schirato & Danaher 2002). In educational settings, Johansson (2007) proposes that these changes can be *vertical* in nature, for example, from home to early childhood service, preschool to primary school, primary school to secondary school, and so on, as well as transitions between classes and teachers within a particular setting. Vertical transitions are usually linked to children's increasing ages, stages of schooling or changes in geographic location. In contrast, transitions can also be *horizontal*, characterised by frequent changes in relatively short time frames typically associated with daily life, such as the move between the social networks of school, outside-school-hours-care, extra-curricula activities and home. Successful transition should build on children's resilience, resourcefulness and relationships with others and 'should result in a child who feels strong and competent, and able to handle new experiences with confidence' (Brooker 2002: 12). In this book, the key focus is on the vertical transition from preschool into the first year of formal schooling.

Contemporary research and policy around transition to school have been influenced by different theories, issues of cultural understanding, equity and social justice, recognition of the rights of the child and children's agency and increased emphasis on the importance of parents and families. Understanding the role of, and developing, links with others is an important part of transition and an opportunity for building *communitas* through shared experiences (Turner 1969). In building *communitas* it is important to recognise the collective and individual vulnerabilities associated with participation and marginalisation (Garpelin 2003, 2004).

The (bio)ecological model of development (Bronfenbrenner 1979, 1986; Bronfenbrenner & Morris 2006) has contributed strongly to the recognition that transitions are complex. This model acknowledges that humans do not develop in isolation, but in relation to the contexts and environments of family and home, school, community and wider society. The complex, ever-changing 'layers' of these environments or ecosystems, and the interactions within and among them, influence an individual's development. 'Each person lives within a micro-system, inside a meso-system, embedded in an exo-system, all of which are part of the macro-system – like a set of concentric circles, nested one inside the other' (Woolfolk & Margetts 2013: 25). In addition, the chrono-system helps explain the influence of normative and non-normative life cycle events overtime such as transitions, personal trauma and socio-historical events.

Transition and change occur 'whenever a person's position in the ecological environment is altered as the result of a change in role, setting, or both' (Bronfenbrenner 1979: 26). As children move between two environments such as the family setting (primary developmental context) and the school setting (secondary developmental context), the process of transition requires meeting the demands of these two microsystem-level environments. The differences between the requirements of these settings may invite displays of the problems related to adjustment in early childhood. The course of a child's early transitions can become a pattern for further ecological transitions and the ability of the child to function in different environments (Bronfenbrenner 1986).

Changes in one ecosystem can lead to changes to the role of an individual and their identity, with possible long-term consequences. A number of chapters in this book focus on changes at the policy level – the macro- and exo-system levels – that involve dominant beliefs, legislation, local authorities and providers, and the impetus for these changes and impact at the micro- and meso-system levels.

What also emerges from these chapters is the role of the chrono-system and the impact of socio-historical events such as economic depression, new emphases in political accountability and personal events on other systems. These temporal dimensions help us to understand long-term practices and traditions and their impact on how change is initially received but also provide insight into the new stages that changes are bringing about in education. Other chapters consider the impact of micro-system changes for children and families as they enter the school system.

An emphasis on human rights and particularly the United Nations Convention on the Rights of the Child (UNCRC) (United Nations High Commission for Human Rights 1989), which incorporates the Declaration of Human Rights (1948), has promoted a focus on: children's agency and the image of children as strong and powerful – 'shall assure to the child who is capable of forming his or her own views the right to express those views freely in all matters affecting the child' (UNCRC, Article 12); respect for family, cultural and other identities of the child; and increased recognition of the role of parents, families and collaborative partnerships for children's well-being, development and learning. A chapter in this book considers policies of social inclusion and the challenges for teachers of meeting the needs of diverse learners. While many governments recognise the important role of parents, Brooker (2002) has suggested that in reality, at the school and practitioner level, home–school relationships are often one-way and schools rarely make provision for teachers to have time to listen to parent perspectives beyond formally scheduled parent–teacher interviews. Two chapters in this book consider children's views about starting school and how these views at the micro-system level can inform policy practice in other ecological systems. Other chapters address parents' responses to transition practices, and how they experience the transition to being the parent of a school child.

Associated with the increased emphasis across the world on early childhood education and care, there is also a focus on outcomes and school readiness – social, cultural, emotional, communication and academic. Two chapters address these issues: one describes strategies for supporting children's literacy competencies using a dialogical approach, while the other considers the socio-emotional and communication aspects.

As with any passages, the success of children's transition to school lies not only in the child's personal characteristics and experiences, but also in the planning and preparation and the readiness of schools and teachers to accept and embrace the diversity that children and their families bring with them. The aspirational *Transition to School: Position Statement* (Educational Transitions and Change (ETC) Research Group 2011) developed by some of the authors represented in this book and other international researchers reflects contemporary research and understandings about transition to school and recognises starting school as a time of aspirations, expectations, opportunities and entitlements.

This book focuses on contemporary international issues and perspectives associated with children and their families making the transition to primary school, and the identification of challenges and changes to beliefs, policy, curriculum and practice. It is framed around the notion of transition as a time of change for those involved in the transition process and as a time for reconceptualising beliefs, policy and practice. The book aims to provide information and raise issues about how transition to school is conceived in different countries and addressed through:

- policy, curriculum frameworks and practice;
- outcomes of children and how children perceive and respond to transition;
- the roles, expectations and experiences of families;
- the implications for change.

It brings together the contemporary work of key researchers from Australia, Denmark, England, Germany, Iceland, Ireland, Poland and Scotland that extends previous research and perspectives and provides empirical evidence to support further development of policy and practice.

Policy, curriculum frameworks and practice

Part II of the book commences with a chapter by Mary O'Kane that provides historical and social/economic background to the Irish context in terms of the policy influences on preschool and primary school environments in 2012 and implications for transition to school. In seeking to increase connections between preschool and school, two new national frameworks have been introduced: Síolta, which is the National Quality Framework for Early Education, and Aistear: the Early Childhood Curriculum Framework. Mary outlines other policy changes with implications for children's transition to school, including the Free Preschool Year scheme, reduced capitation and an increase in the child to adult ratio. Mary advocates for the importance of research that has policy as well as practical implications and describes recent projects that support the notion of cost-effectiveness.

In Chapter 3, Anna Kienig addresses the most significant change in the Polish educational system during the years 2009–2012: the change of the age of compulsory-school entry from 7 to 6 years. Before 2012 parents could send 6-year-old children to school, or to preschool settings, including those in schools ('0' class). Anna describes implications of this and reactions of the Polish community to this and associated changes. She then reports studies undertaken prior to and following the commencement of the reforms, the most recent of which analysed the social competencies of 6-year-old children in different educational settings: preschool, kindergarten and 1st grade. Although the results of the study show differences in the level of socio-emotional functioning among the 6-year-old children from the different types of settings, the results were unexpected and further studies are recommended.

Anne Petriwskyj, in Chapter 4, provides an overview of beliefs that preschool and school teachers hold about transition, the impact of these beliefs on transition and the need for more inclusive practices. She then outlines policy initiatives in Australia, particularly in the state of Queensland, such as changes to school entry age, improvements to early education, and the development of national curriculum documents. While these have aimed to support transition to school, Anne argues that they have proved insufficient to cater for the diversity of school entrants. She then describes some pedagogic initiatives that support transition and maintain continuity of learning between home, community, early childhood services and school.

Outcomes for children and children's perspectives

Hilary Fabian, in Chapter 5, the first chapter in Part III on transition outcomes, identifies some challenges of transition. She then considers how successful transition for children might be achieved particularly in terms of: continuity of learning; social and cultural understanding; emotional well-being; and effective communication. She stresses that schools should have policies in place to support successful transition and these should be reviewed regularly. Hilary concludes with a reminder that transition while undertaken in community is an individual process that needs to be personalised and takes time.

In the following chapter, Anders Skriver Jensen, Ole Henrik Hansen and Stig Broström commence with an overview of the Danish day care and school system, including legislation and policy to ease and optimise the transition to school. The chapter then addresses the importance of day care services in facilitating desired outcomes for children, particularly literacy and language development. In rethinking traditional approaches to early childhood education, Anders, Ole and Stig advocate for an approach that merges pedagogy, which combines the Nordic social–pedagogic tradition with the focus on social competencies and democratic dimensions, with the teaching of reading and writing. They report research about what teachers think about their own pedagogy in relation to early years literacy and describe a dialogic or literature dialogue approach to developing children's literacy.

In Chapter 7, Johanna Einarsdottir describes research that focuses on children's perspectives, expectations and experiences of starting primary school. The chapter builds on four studies conducted with children in preschools and primary schools in Iceland. The first study reports children's expectations about school prior to commencement. A further study identifies how children regarded their preparation for school and the associated changes. Following their commencement at school, two studies report children's views about the actual differences they found between preschool and school, and their perspectives about their influence on the school curriculum. Findings reveal important perspectives and disconnections related to status and responsibility, teaching methods, democracy, learning and social relationships.

In recognising the importance of children's agency and their role in contributing to matters that involve them, Kay Margetts in Chapter 8 considers the perspectives of children in the first year of school in Victoria, Australia, about what new entrant children need to know as they start school and what they think schools can do to help children starting school. Emerging issues relate to peer relationships, school rules, general procedures, classrooms, academic skills and emotions and feelings. The links between these issues and what schools can do to assist new entrant children were very strong, and provided evidence for the validity of children's suggestions for dealing with issues that affect children commencing school.

Roles, expectations and experiences of families

The notion that transitions are distinctive socially embedded transformation processes of children and their families that are mastered by intensified learning processes of each person going through the transition is presented in Chapter 9 by Wilfried Griebel and Renate Niesel. Based on transition theory modelled in the field of family developmental psychology, Wilfried and Renate explain transitions as critical life events that promote development in terms of restructuring one's psychological sense of self and a shift in one's assumptive world. They then report research about the many changes that parents had to deal with during their own transitions to being parents of a school child. In considering how schools can foster school–family partnerships, they conclude the chapter with a challenge for nursery schools and schools to consider the extent to which they respond to parents' different life circumstances and needs, rather than expecting the parents to change.

Sue Dockett and Bob Perry, in Chapter 10, consider the role of families and communities in the transition to school and how, during this time of change, relationships between parents and teachers are important for children's success. Referring to the recent *Transition to School: Position Statement* (Educational Transitions and Change (ETC) Research Group 2011), which reconceptualises transition to school as being characterised by opportunities, aspirations, expectations and entitlements for all involved, they identify what these characteristics mean for families. This is followed by an examination of the experiences of one family during the transition to school and how they were afforded opportunities, how aspirations were promoted, expectations generated and entitlements identified, rather than a focus on increased vulnerability and risk.

In Chapter 11, Divya Jindal-Snape and Elizabeth Hannah provide a brief overview of the Scottish Early Years Framework in which there is a strong focus on the role and contribution of parents and families. They report a study in a local authority in Scotland to map the perspectives of 73 parents about their experiences of early years transition practice onto the recommendations of an Integrated Services Task Group report that informed the content of The Early

Years Framework. Suggestions are made about how transition policy and practice can be reconceptualised to better address parental participation.

Reframing transition and curriculum

There has been a strong focus on the need to prepare children for school, to support them in their adjustment to school and more recently to advocate the need for schools to change their practices to be 'child ready' so that the changes children need to make to accommodate new experiences are better matched by practices in the new school. In Chapter 12, Aline-Wendy Dunlop reflects on early years curriculum and considers whether curriculum itself can be a tool for change in transition practices – or perhaps the converse, that transitions are a tool for changing curriculum that has not been serving young children well. Such changes within schools may mean a more individualised approach to children and families, an appreciation of differences between children and parents as well as between systems. Aline-Wendy suggests that where preschools and schools operate together in more tightly coupled systems it is expected that the demands placed on children are more manageable for them.

Finally

In Chapter 13 we bring together the issues that have been presented in preceding chapters and implications for reconceptualising beliefs, policy and practice around transition to school.

References

Bronfenbrenner, U. (1979) *The Ecology of Human Development: Experiments by Nature and Design*, Cambridge: Harvard University Press.

Bronfenbrenner, U. (1986) 'Ecology of the family as a context for human development: research perspectives', *Developmental Psychology* 22: 723–733.

Bronfenbrenner, U. and Morris, P.A. (2006) 'The bioecological model of human development', in R.M. Lerner (ed.) *Theoretical Models of Human Development* (Volume 1 of *Handbook of Child Psychology*, 6th edn.) (pp. 793–828), Hoboken, NJ: Wiley.

Brooker, L. (2002) *Starting School: Young Children Learning Culture*, Buckingham: Open University Press.

Campbell Clark, S. (2000) 'Work/family border theory: A new theory of work/family balance, *Human Relations* 53(6): 747–770.

Educational Transitions and Change (ETC) Research Group (2011) *Transition to School: Position Statement*, Albury-Wodonga: Research Institute for Professional Practice, Learning and Education, Charles Sturt University.

Elder, G.H., Jr. (1998) 'The lifecourse as developmental theory', *Child Development* 69(1): 1–12.

Garpelin, A. (2003) *Ung i Skolan* (Young in School), Lund: Studentlitteratur.

Garpelin, A. (2004) 'Accepted or rejected in school', *European Educational Research Journal* 3(4): 729–742.

Johannson, I. (2007) 'Horizontal transitions: What can it mean for children in the early school years?', in A.-W. Dunlop and H. Fabian (eds.) *Informing Transitions in the Early Years* (pp. 33–44), Berkshire: Open University Press.

Turner, V. (1969) *The Ritual Process: Structure and Anti-Structure*, London: Routledge & Kegan Paul.

United Nations (1989) *Convention on the Rights of the Child*. Online, available at: <http://www2.ohchr.org/english/law/crc.htm> (accessed 18 September 2012).

van Gennep, A. (1960) *The Rites of Passage*, Chicago: University of Chicago Press.

Webb, J., Schirato, T. and Danaher, G. (2002) *Understanding Bourdieu*, London: Sage.

Woolfolk, A. and Margetts, K. (2013) *Educational Psychology* (3rd edn.), Frenchs Forrest: Pearson Australia.

PART II

Policy, curriculum frameworks and practice

2

THE TRANSITION FROM PRESCHOOL TO PRIMARY SCHOOL IN IRELAND

A time of change

Mary O'Kane

Researchers have emphasised the importance of placing the transition from preschool to primary school in the context of the historical and social environment in which the transition is taking place, stressing the need to look at the multi-level systems that influence children during this time (Bronfenbrenner & Morris 1998; Elder 2007). Fulcher (2007) agrees that historical and cross-cultural meanings are important to consider when viewing transitions in the lives of children, and places great emphasis on the local–regional policy environment. With this in mind, this chapter provides a background to the Irish context in terms of the policy influences on preschool and primary school environments in 2012 and how these impact on the educational transition.

The Irish context

The Republic of Ireland underwent a period of rapid economic growth from 1995 to 2007 known as the 'Celtic Tiger'. During this time an increasing involvement of women in the workplace led to a greater demand for preschool provision and state support became a political issue. However, this economic growth underwent a dramatic reversal in 2008 when economic activity dropped sharply. Ireland then entered into a recession that is currently impacting on every area of Irish life, including education, with concern being expressed at both preschool and primary level about the impact of government cuts on educational services (Early Childhood Ireland 2012; Irish National Teachers Organisation (INTO) 2012).

Preschool provision in Ireland relates to any early childhood care and education (ECCE) setting that caters for children up to 6 years of age, apart from primary schools. Historically state involvement was principally limited to provision of places for children seen to be at risk. However, during the Celtic

Tiger period unprecedented investment into the area of ECCE was made under the EU-funded *Equal Opportunities Childcare Programme* (EOCP) and its successor the *National Childcare Investment Programme* (NCIP). Both schemes have resulted in quality improvement; nonetheless it is asserted that even in this boom period investment was driven by political goals with regard to market-based capacity increases rather than quality objectives (Hayes & Bradley 2009).

Compulsory education in Ireland begins at the age of 6 years; however, many children in the Republic start school as young as 4 years of age (Office for Early Childhood Development (OECD) 2004). The first-entrants class is called the Junior Infant class, and usually commences on the first of September each year. The kind of educational experiences that 4-year-olds are receiving in Irish infant classrooms and whether appropriate play-based learning experiences can be provided in these classes with current adult:child ratios and large class sizes has been questioned (O'Kane 2007a). The most recent OECD report on Ireland (2004) cited that 54 per cent of Junior Infant pupils are in classes of between 25 and 34 children, which would be classed as unacceptable in most other European countries. Indeed, INTO (2012) highlight continuing concerns about the impact of budget cuts on class sizes. It has been asserted that Irish primary school classrooms are teacher-focused rather than child-friendly, with outdated design and facilities, unsuitable for modern teaching and learning (Darmody, Smyth & Doherty 2010).

The commonalities between *how* children learn in both preschool and Junior Infant settings call for similar learning environments and teaching strategies. Instead of working towards continuity, the differences between the preschool and primary school sectors in Ireland are emphasised by differences in almost every aspect of operation: curricula, staff training, regulation and inspection, historical and cultural differences. There is also no national policy in Ireland for transitions; indeed O'Kane (2007a) reported that very few formal policies or practices with regard to transition are being implemented at ground level. However, two new frameworks have been introduced at a national level and it is hoped that they will increase connections in quality experiences and learning throughout early childhood. These are *Síolta*, the *National Quality Framework for Early Education* (Centre for Early Childhood Development and Education (CECDE) 2006) and *Aistear: the Early Childhood Curriculum Framework* (National Council for Curriculum and Assessment (NCCA) 2009).

Síolta and Aistear

In terms of policy associated with the transition from preschool to primary school in Ireland, both *Síolta* and *Aistear* have important implications, focusing both on the contexts for learning and the principles of learning. In the absence of any formal national policy on transitions they can be viewed as a step towards developing cross-sectoral links.

Síolta is a set of national quality standards for early childhood education, covering services for children from birth to 6 years (covering both preschool services and the infant classes). The framework identifies 12 interdependent principles of quality that outline the vision behind the framework. From these principles, 16 national standards cover the actual areas of practice to be addressed. These are further broken down into components of quality for practitioners to use as quality indicators. The aim is that the principles, standards and components when used together form a coherent basis for quality achievement. Settings may also implement a full *Síolta Quality Assurance Programme* that provides structured, supported engagement for services seeking assessment against the *Síolta Standards*. The framework should enable a positive progression in terms of working towards quality in ECCE services in a coordinated and cohesive way. Anecdotal evidence suggests that although there is good involvement at preschool level, it is not being implemented to any great extent in primary schools (O'Kane & Hayes 2010).

A complementary framework, which can be used in tandem with *Síolta*, is *Aistear*. While *Síolta* provides national standards for quality, focusing on the contexts in which children learn, *Aistear* focuses on curriculum and learning opportunities providing principles for learning. This framework also covers children from birth to age 6 in early childhood settings in Ireland, including the infant classes of primary schools. Four interconnected themes have been identified within *Aistear*: well-being; identity and belonging; communicating; and exploring and thinking. The framework provides information for adults to help them plan for and provide enjoyable and challenging learning experiences for the children in their care. It describes the types of learning (dispositions, values, skills, knowledge and understanding) that are important for children in their early years, and offers ideas and suggestions as to how this learning might be nurtured. *Aistear* is intended to complement existing curricular material and support a progression in learning from preschool through to primary school in terms of curriculum.

The implementation of such frameworks should create greater coherence across the two learning settings, and in order to support children making the transition from preschool to the primary school system greater engagement across both sectors is important. One concern is that adherence to both is voluntary at present. The reality of how practitioners in both sectors make use of the two frameworks has yet to become apparent.

Free Preschool Year

Another important policy implication for the transition from preschool to primary in Ireland is the *Free Preschool Year* (Office of the Minister for Children 2010) scheme, which commenced in 2010. The reason for the introduction of the scheme is important to note. In a time of recession the scheme replaced the *Early Childhood Supplement* (ECS), which was a payment made to families with children under 5 years old to assist with the costs of raising children, such as childcare costs. The ECS cost the Government €480 million a year while the *Free Preschool Year* is estimated to cost the Government €170 million annually (Gartland 2010). Although the scheme has been widely welcomed by the ECCE sector in terms of the entitlement of children to a year of free preschool, it has been criticised in terms of its introduction without planning and consultation. Indeed, the ECS itself was criticised when it was introduced in 2006, as the decision to commence that payment contravened all policy advice at the time, corroborating the theory that ECCE policy decisions in Ireland are guided by political goals and not a drive for quality (Bradley 2010).

The *Free Preschool Year* scheme allows children enrolled in playschools to receive free preschool provision of 3 hours per day, 5 days each week over a 38-week year. Participating children must normally be more than 3 years 2 months and less than 4 years 7 months in the September they commence the scheme. Concern has been identified that the age limits identified by the scheme will act as a 'recommendation' by the Government to parents as to when a child is ready to start school (O'Kane & Hayes 2010). A child starting the free preschool year at 3 years 2 months would therefore start school at 4 years 2 months, while practitioners have been calling for some time to have the school starting age in Ireland raised to 5 years. The same report identified a concern among practitioners that parents already focus on age of the child rather than skill sets at this time when making decisions about when to send their child to school.

From September 2012, the government will reduce the capitation paid to preschools and increase the adult:child ratio for the scheme from 1:10 to 1:11. Once again this measure is an economic one. Anecdotal evidence suggests some concerns about the impact of this decision on practitioners and the children in their care in terms of these cuts impacting on the quality of care provided (Harding 2012). Early Childhood Ireland has reported in a recent member survey a projected shortfall of income to costs of €13 million for 2012 (Gunning 2011), which practitioners advise will hinder their ability to provide a quality service.

Irish research into the transition from preschool to primary

During this time of recession, it is particularly important for researchers to make links between research and practice to inform policy development. The focus on transition to formal schooling has increased dramatically in Ireland in recent years. O'Kane (2007a) provided the first national data on the policies and procedures in use in Irish preschools and schools with regard to the transition to school, and since that date further work has been undertaken (Doyle, Logue & McNamara 2009; O'Kane & Hayes 2010; Preparing for Life Group 2006). If children in Ireland are to benefit from the past investment made into ECCE and capitalise on it at primary level, there is a clear need to work towards stronger supports as they make the transition from one educational environment to the other. The research described below aims to provide information that can impact in a practical way on children undergoing this transition, while also providing data for use in policy development.

The 'Building Bridges' study (O'Kane 2007a, 2009) was the first major research project into the transition from preschool to primary school in Ireland. It investigated the beliefs of both preschool and primary school practitioners about the process, and examined the transition from the perspective of children undergoing the transition and their parents. The study found a lack of communication in the study between Irish preschools and primary schools, suggesting that there was little congruence in approaches to learning. It was suggested that the two groups of teachers have only a limited understanding of each other's working ideologies and environments. However, both groups advised that they were open to greater communication. Both also agreed that children with the ability to negotiate classroom life independently, equipped with good social skills and the ability to concentrate and listen for short periods of time, are more likely to be successful at primary level (O'Kane 2007b; O'Kane & Hayes 2006). It was suggested that a difference between rhetoric and reality exists however; for example, the skills of acting independently and the ability to sit and listen were both highly valued, which is a difficult balance for children of this age to achieve.

The children themselves noted a loss of independence during the transition, with an emphasis on obedience and compliance, and a lack of autonomy noted in the role of school child. It was clear that opportunities for sustained shared thinking were limited in the infant classes of primary school. Class size, adult:child ratios, the lack of appropriate training in play-based philosophies and time for reflection were noted as being challenges to the development of a more play-based practice.

The issue of cultural capital being transferred across the home–school environments was also apparent. The findings of the study concur with the notion that transition to school is an adaptive process for children and their families, and that all stakeholders should be involved in communication about the process (O'Kane 2007a; O'Kane & Hayes 2008).

Overall study findings reported that the beliefs, expectations and classroom practices of both preschool and primary school teachers have a great impact on transition. Low levels of continuity and planning for transition were identified. Indeed, a lack of understanding in both sectors as to the extent and nature of the other providers' services was noted. It was suggested that in order for a co-construction of transition to take place between the two groups of teachers there needed to be a mutual clarification of expectations, a clearer understanding of meanings and greater levels of communication and consistency between the two educational spheres.

Communication and collaboration between educational settings

Following on from that research, O'Kane and Hayes (2010) further investigated some of these issues in a designated disadvantaged area in Dublin. This project involved two primary schools and 12 feeder preschools, with a specific focus on developing processes for communication and collaboration between the two educational settings, pedagogy and curriculum, and enhancing parental involvement.

In order to address the issues of lack of communication and coordination between the two educational settings, a 'Child Snapshot' form was developed by staff from both sectors as a tool for the transfer of information on children from preschool to primary school. This form was designed to capture the rich knowledge base developed at preschool level and facilitate its efficient transfer across to the primary sector. The development process involved a mutual clarification of expectations, in terms of the skill sets that support children making the transition to school, and an investigation into the professional language used in the two sectors. Engagement in the process itself was seen as an integral part of the collaboration between the two settings. Formal evaluation of the project found that participants were overwhelmingly positive about the Child Snapshot in terms of transfer of information, as a tool to communicate with parents during this transition and in terms of the benefits of professional collaboration.

A Continuing Professional Development (CPD) programme was also an important part of the project. The focus that the CPD would take was decided during consultation with both groups of practitioners. It was agreed that the two main areas of importance were: curriculum and pedagogy; and child and parental engagement. These two modules included sessions on developing oral language and mathematical concepts; a focus on play as a learning tool in various aspects of development; and practical and psychological support for parents and children during this transition. All 12 preschools took part in the CPD. The pilot programme ran over a two-week period, and was formally evaluated with a view to further development. As an offshoot of the CPD, a 'Programme for Developing Mathematical Concepts in Preschools' and a 'Tips for Parents of Children Starting School' booklet were also developed, which continue to be used in the preschool settings.

Recommendations from the project included nationwide application of the Child Snapshot; indeed the tool has since been used as an example of best practice, which has been modelled for development in another designated disadvantaged area in Dublin. It was noted as being a very cost-effective way to support children, parents and practitioners during transition. Both the CPD and the 'Tips for Parents' booklet have been recommended for further development, again noted as being cost-effective measures to implement. Finally it was recommended that more coordinated structures be put into place nationally to facilitate communication between the two sectors. This would enhance the quality of the transition experience for children through curricular and pedagogical continuity and thus strengthen the impact of the preschool experience.

It was highlighted during the course of this project that the introduction of the *Free Preschool Year* for children will see more children from disadvantaged areas attending preschool settings. To maximise the positive impact of quality preschool experiences, supports for the transition to the primary school environment need to be set in place. The project report noted that the benefits gained during early intervention may not automatically transfer to the new school context and there is a need to support children's adjustment during this time. The outcomes from this research study provided a timely contribution to developments in this critical aspect of early childhood education.

Conclusion

Following on from the research described above we are beginning to more clearly understand this transition in the Irish context. The research provides evidence that should be used by policy makers to develop cost-effective support systems to facilitate smooth transitions from preschool to primary school. It is clear when considering the impact of the local–regional policy environment as recommended by Fulcher (2007) that the *Free Preschool Year* initiative, *Síolta* and *Aistear* are currently exerting an external force on the organisational context in which our children are operating. The impact of these supports will only become evident in time. However, it is apparent that in 2012 this is not only a transition for the individual children and their families, but is also a time of transition to a new educational landscape for all stakeholders in the process.

References

Bradley, S. (2010) 'Behind closed doors: Exploring the experiences of key voices in Irish ECEC policy making'. Paper presented at 20th EECERA Conference, Birmingham, UK, 6–8 September, 2010.

Bronfenbrenner, U. and Morris, P.A. (1998) 'The ecology of developmental processes', in W. Damon and R.M. Lerner (eds.) *Handbook of Child Psychology: Vol. 1. Theoretical Models of Human Development* (5th edn., pp. 993–1029), Hoboken, NJ: John Wiley & Sons.

Centre for Early Childhood Development and Education (CECDE) (2006) *Síolta, the National Quality Framework for Early Childhood Education Handbook*, Dublin: CECDE.

Darmody, M., Smyth, M. and Doherty, C. (2010) *Designing Primary Schools for the Future. Research Series No.16*, Dublin: Economic and Social Research Institute.

Doyle, O., Logue, C. and McNamara, K. (2009) 'Readiness for change: Evidence from a study of early childhood care and education centres', *UCD Geary Institute Working Paper*, Dublin: University College Dublin, Geary Institute.

Early Childhood Ireland (2012) *Pre-Budget Submission November 2012*. Online, available at: <http://www.earlychildhoodireland.ie/policy-advocacy-and-research/pre-budget-submissions/> (accessed July 2012).

Elder, G.H., Jr. (2007) 'Bringing context to human development – a tribute to Urie Bronfenbrenner'. Keynote address at 'Transforming Transitions', International Transitions Research Conference, University of Strathclyde, Glasgow, 11–13 April 2007.

Fulcher, L. (2007) 'Re-thinking transitions and cross-cultural meaning making in a rapidly changing society'. Keynote address at 'Transforming Transitions', International Transitions Research Conference, University of Strathclyde, Glasgow, 11–13 April 2007.

Gartland, F. (2010) *94% of Eligible Children Available of Free Pre-school Year*, Dublin: Irish Times.

Gunning, I. (2011) *In My Opinion: Ministers, Do Your Homework and Extend the Free Preschool Scheme*. Online, available at: <http://www.independent.ie/lifestyle/education/features/in-my-opinion-ministers-do-your-homework-and-extend-free-preschool-scheme-2942456.html> (accessed April 2012).

Harding, L. (2012) 'Childcare in Ireland today'. Unpublished Student Research Project, College of Progressive Education, Dublin.

Hayes, N. and Bradley, S. (2009) *Right by Children: Rights-Based Approaches to Policy Making in Early Childhood Education and Care: The Case of Ireland*, Dublin: Centre for Social and Educational Research/Dublin Institute of Technology.

Irish National Teachers Organisation (INTO) (2012) *INTO in the Media*. Online, available at: <http://www.into.ie/ROI/NewsEvents/MediaCoverage/January2012/> (accessed May 2012).

National Council for Curriculum and Assessment (NCCA) (2009) *Aistear: the Early Childhood Curriculum Framework*. Online, available at: <http://www.ncca.ie/en/Curriculum_and_Assessment/Early_Childhood_and_Primary_Education/Early_Childhood_Education/> (accessed April 2012).

Office for Early Childhood Development (OECD) (2004) *OECD Thematic Review of Early Childhood Education and Care Policy in Ireland*, Dublin: The Stationery Office.

Office of the Minister for Children (2010) *Terms and Conditions, Free Preschool Year in Early Childhood Care and Education (ECCE) Scheme*. Online, available at: <http://www.omc.gov.ie/viewdoc.asp?fn=/documents/childcare/ECCE_Scheme_Pack/Terms_and_Conditions_ECCE_Sept_2010.doc> (accessed April 2012).

O'Kane, M. (2007a) 'Building bridges: The transition from preschool to primary school for children in Ireland'. Unpublished PhD Thesis, Dublin Institute of Technology.

O'Kane, M. (2007b) 'The transition to school in Ireland: What do the children say?'. Paper presented at the International Transitions Research Conference, University of Strathclyde, Glasgow, Scotland, 11–13 April 2007.

O'Kane, M. (2009) 'The transition from preschool to primary school in Ireland: Views of primary school teachers', in INTO (2009) *INTO Consultative Conference on Education 2008, Transitions in the Primary School. Final Report*, Dublin: INTO.

O'Kane, M. and Hayes, N. (2006) 'The transition to school in Ireland: Views of preschool and primary school teachers', *International Journal of Transitions in Childhood* 2: 4–16.

O'Kane, M. and Hayes, N. (2008) 'The transition to school in Ireland: What do the children say?'. *Proceedings of the CECDE International Conference 'Vision into Practice: Making Quality a Reality in the Lives of Young Children'*, Dublin: CECDE.

O'Kane, M. and Hayes, N. (2010) *Supporting Early Childhood Educational Provision Within a Cluster of DEIS Preschool and Primary School Settings with a Specific Focus on Transition Between the Two Educational Settings*, Dublin: Centre for Social and Educational Research, Dublin Institute of Technology/Department of Education and Science.

Preparing for Life Group (2006) *Preparing for Life: Planning Together for our Children. A Report on School Readiness in the Communities of Belcamp, Darndale and Moatview*, Dublin: Preparing for Life Group/Northside Partnership.

3

CHILDREN'S TRANSITION FROM KINDERGARTEN TO PRIMARY SCHOOL

Anna Kienig

The most important challenge in the Polish educational system during the years 2009–2012 has been the change of the age of compulsory-school entry: from 7 to 6 years. Before 2012 parents could send 6-year-old children to school, or to preschool settings, including those in schools ('0' class). The bio-ecological perspective conceives transition to school as an ecological change in life, which involves changes in identity, roles and relationships. In coping with these changes, researchers have identified different social competencies that children need: self-reliance, problem-solving and coping with stress. A study undertaken in the first year of the reform analysed the social competencies of 6-year-old children in different educational settings: preschool, kindergarten and 1st grade. The results of the study show differences in the level of socio-emotional functioning among the 6-year-old children from the different types of institutions.

Introduction: Polish context

Until the year 2009, all children aged 3–6 years were included in preschool education in Poland. Preschool education was provided either in preschool settings operating as independent institutions, or as kindergarten classes functioning within the framework of primary schools. According to a long tradition, 7-year-olds would begin their education in the first class of primary school. The basic problem in the education of young children in Poland has for a long time been a low rate of participation in preschool education – in the year 2002 only 52 per cent of 3–6-year-old children attended preschool settings (36 per cent were aged 3–5 and 97 per cent were 6-year-olds). The main goal of the 2009 educational system reform was to increase participation in kindergarten education and to lower the age of compulsory school attendance from 7 to 6 years of age in order to equalise children's chances of future success.

The change to school entry associated with the 2009/2011 reforms by the Department of Education were designed to be phased in over three school years. Beginning with the school year 2009/2010, children aged 6 years could commence their education in the first grade of primary school or they could remain in kindergarten. However, from 1 October 2012 there was to be no choice and all 6-year-olds were expected to commence school. During the transitory period, decisions about whether a child should begin formal education have been the responsibility of each child's parents and the school head-teacher, including that: the school ensures appropriate organisation of learning and standards of premises; the child has had at least a year-long period during which they attended kindergarten; and they have received an assessment estimating the level of development.

Lowering the age of compulsory school attendance to the sixth year of life is also connected with including all 5-year-olds in compulsory kindergarten education in preschool education (a preschool group) preparatory to starting school commencing in the 2011/2012 school year.

The data show that only 4 per cent of 6-year-old children commenced Grade 1 in 2009/2012 and in the following year 2010/2011 this rose slightly to 10 per cent (www.men.gov.pl).

Changing the age at which children begin compulsory education has sparked many controversies among parents, teachers and educational authorities. An example of the determination of the parents protesting the lowering of compulsory schooling/education age are spectacular actions such as the 'Save the kiddies' initiative and the creation of civic action proposing the bringing back of the age of 7 years for commencing compulsory schooling, signed by several thousand people. Parental anxiety has related mainly to concerns that school premises and the organisation of the curriculum may be inadequate for 6-year-olds, including overemphasis on academic learning and limited focus on social and emotional development. The advocates of lowering the age for compulsory schooling point to the example of most European countries, where children as young as 6 years, and even younger, begin their formal education. Controversies surrounding the lowering of the compulsory school entry age resulted in a change in the law, and in delaying the completion of the process until the year 2014.

Starting school as educational transition

Transitions have been defined as phases of life changes connected with developmental demands that require intensified and accelerated learning and that are socially regulated (Griebel & Niesel 2005). Transitions can be periods of intensified and accelerated developmental change, influenced by social situations and contexts involving environment, social and cognitive learning as well as emotional turmoil (Fabian & Dunlop 2005).

Educational transition is the process of change that takes place when children move from one place or phase of education to another (Fabian & Dunlop 2002).

Starting school has been perceived as one of the most important transitions in a child's life and a major challenge of early childhood (Fabian & Dunlop 2006).

According to Bronfenbrenner's (1979) ecological theory of human development, transition to school involves ecological changes in life including changes in identity, roles and relationships. A child beginning school must rise to the many challenges posed by the change of their social environment, the necessity of mastering a new style of learning and adapting to educational demands as well as to the norms and customs that govern the school life. Simultaneous changes in social relationships, teachers' teaching style, the physical environment and contexts for teaching and learning intensify the challenges facing the child, and are related to an acceleration in developmental demands (Fabian & Dunlop 2005). This can lead to multiple difficulties in the initial phase of the child's school education, interfering with their functioning in the role of a primary school student. Anna Brzezińska and Tomasz Czub (1991) point to the discrepancy between the child's previous experiences and their image of social relationships and the reality of school as another reason for children's difficulties.

Children whose cultural environments of home and school are similar deal more easily with starting school. The children who perceive the school as alien and different from their home context tend to experience difficulties, to complicate educational and social situations and to experience fear during educational transition, particularly when there are marked differences between these environments. The difference can also pertain to low cultural capital of those children's families (Szlendak 2003) or their low educational aspirations (Murawska 2004). An important role in a child's start to school is also played by communication and cooperation between all the people involved – parents, kindergarten and school teachers (Broström 2002; Dunlop 2002).

Brzezińska, Matejczuk and Nowotnik (2012: 12) analysed the school readiness of 5- and 6-year-olds and the 'readiness' of the school to accept children who, as a result of the education reforms in Poland, are younger than they used to be. They redefined the role and tasks of adults (parents and teachers) in the process of the child's transition to school, emphasising that preparing children for school consists primarily of fostering a child's development from the earliest age: building personal resources during childhood and developing competencies connected to the process of learning and particular competencies relevant to fulfilling school tasks. The researchers have defined broad aims that are important to successful learning at school:

- short-term aims – preparing the child to cope with the tests set forth in the first grade: reading; writing; interacting with peers and the teacher; independent activity;
- medium-term aims – preparing the child for the process of school education and for *lifelong learning:* building competencies connected to learning; organising study; taking responsibility for one's own learning and development;

- long-term aims – preparing the child to participate in the complex social and informational reality.

Lowering the age at which children begin compulsory school education is thus viewed as a challenge not only for the children but, most of all, for their parents and teachers.

A number of researchers have identified a range of developmental challenges or crises that children beginning school are faced with (e.g. Havighurst, 1972). According to Griebel and Niesel (2003) they include the following aspects: individual, interactional and contextual.

Vygotsky (1972 cited in Brzezińska, Appelt & Ziółkowska 2008) described the crisis of the sixth to seventh year of life as connected with the appearance of the so-called intellectual moment accompanied by a breakdown in emotional balance and a changeability of mood, as well as a dysfunction of will. Simultaneously, it is this period that sees the development of the child's independence and positive relationships with other children. According to Erikson (1968 cited in Brzezińska, Appelt & Ziółkowska 2008) the beginning of school education coincides with the child moving into the fourth developmental phase (industry versus guilt), which occurs between 6 and 12 years of age. It is an important stage in the development of the child's independence (from a gradual loosening of the bond with their parents towards adult independence) and a broadening of the sphere of social interactions. The positive side of the developmental process in this period is the rise in the sense of competence, adequacy and productivity, while the main threats are the sense of inferiority and excessive adequacy and properness. Erikson (1968 cited in Stefańska-Klar 2000) emphasised that the danger of this period is the drive to at all costs meet the demands set before the child, mainly their school duties. The child can become dependent on the tasks set before them and, in the future, become convinced that the sole criterion of human value is the ability to meet demands. Thus the new challenges and developmental tasks faced by a child during their educational transition to the first grade of primary school demand from them an increased adaptive effort. What can act as a factor facilitating a child's school start is their high level of social competence.

Social competence

In the psychological and pedagogical literature there are many definitions of the notion of 'social competence'. As noted by H. Rudolph Schaffer (2010), this notion belongs among the most poorly defined and ambivalent. The notion of social competence is most often equated with social abilities, although some authors propose that we should distinguish between skills/behaviours and outcomes. In doing this, the analysis by Hubbard and Coie (1994) identified that, as sets of skills, social competencies comprised behaviours such as empathy, eagerness to cooperate, willingness to offer help, skills connected to interactional play and conversational abilities. Social competencies as the aims and outcomes of such behaviours include popularity among peers, having friends,and acquiring influence on others. Defining social competence in these two ways supports the notion of social competence as the ability to achieve social aims, engage in complex social interactions, strike up and keep friendships, become group members and gain peer acceptance (Denham 1998; Eisenberg & Fabes 1992 cited in Kielar–Turska 2011).

Social competencies are closely connected to emotional competencies and together enable effective functioning in social situations (Brzezińska 2005; Schaffer 2005). Halberstadt, Dunsmore and Denham (2001) have proposed the term *affective social competence* – emotional skills are basic in successful social interactions.

Psychological and pedagogical literature describes a range of social skills that support children in the process of transition to new environments (Fabian 2002; Griebel & Niesel 2002; Margetts 2002b): the ability to establish social relationships with children and adults to cooperate with others, coping in difficult situations, a sense of autonomy and well-being. What is especially emphasised is the role of the sense of emotional well-being in helping children to cope in a new social context (Broström 2002; Bulkeley & Fabian 2006; Griebel & Niesel 2002).

Beginning formal school education is also a chance to enlarge the scope of one's social competences – of acquiring social rules and values and of transforming one's identity, roles and relations (Griebel & Niesel 2002; Kienig 2005).

Children's and parents' knowledge and expectations towards school

Similar to studies in other countries (Dockett & Perry 2007; Einarsdottir 2003; Griebel & Niesel 2002) a number of studies have specifically investigated the perspectives of children and parents in Poland about starting school. Joanna Sikorska (2008) investigated the opinions of 127 6-year-old children from kindergarten groups to identify their knowledge and expectations of school. Sikorska's research shows that children associate learning at school with: obtaining good grades; executing tasks set by the teacher; establishing contacts with peers; and praise received from the teacher. Most of the children (64 per cent) enumerated specific school subjects such as reading, writing and mathematics, but 36 per cent of the children knew only that at school pupils learn to 'read and write', 'learn everything', 'learn how to cross the street' and 'learn how to be good "cause mummy says when you go to school they will teach you some discipline"'.

Nearly all children (95 per cent) associated the role of pupil/student exclusively with duties: 'has to study and listen to the teacher', 'has to answer all kinds of questions', 'has to be good' and 'cannot be late'. In addition, research by Elżbieta Jaszczyszyn (2010) shows that 6-year-old children identify the following tasks associated with being a student: studying (79 per cent); colouring and painting (75 per cent); playing during recess (24 per cent); and listening to the teacher (16 per cent).

Children have pointed out the differences between kindergarten and school (Sikorska 2008): 'at school children study, in the kindergarten they play' (68 per cent), 'at school you can't play, but in the kindergarten you can' (7 per cent) and 'at school you must study, and in the kindergarten you don't' (5 per cent). Most of the children in this study (73 per cent) commented that at school one cannot do the things one feels like doing (that is, play): 'no, because you have to study'; 'you can, but only during recess'; you can do what you feel like doing 'when it is children's day, when it is your birthday'; and 'you cannot play because there are no toys'.

Sikorska (2008) stresses that the positive attitude towards school and the duties inherent in the role of a pupil exhibited by the 6-year-olds in the study come from a positive attitude toward school that is evident in their environment and from these children's systematic preparation for learning at school. Children are happy that they will go to school and they want to learn. It is important that the school is ready to help overcome adaptive barriers.

As well as the perspectives of children about starting school, it is important to understand and respond to parents' expectations towards school (Jaszczyszyn 2010). Parents of 6-year-old children pay attention especially to the material and organisational aspects of school, such as: children are safe and secure; the teaching aids with which the classroom is equipped are varied and appropriate for pupils' ages; the school can provide the child with meals, allows access to a playground and offers care of the child outside the classroom. Less frequently parents point to the teacher's qualifications, which ensure that knowledge is transmitted to pupils in a way that is adapted to each particular child's capacities or that prepares the child for further educational levels. What parents mentioned least frequently was the role of school in developing children's independence, responsibility and self-assurance.

Research associated with the starting school age reforms in Poland

Before taking the decision to lower the age of children starting school, *The Six-Year-Old Child at the Threshold of School Education* (*Dziecko sześcioletnie u progu nauki szkolnej*) study involving 70,000 children was conducted in 2006 financed from the resources provided by the European Social Funds (Kopik 2007) to investigate the development and school readiness of 6-year-old children in kindergarten.

Information was collected about children's physical, motor, cognitive and socio-emotional development, as well as information about health and the environmental and educational conditions in which the child's development takes place. Seventy thousand parents of 6-year-old children, 3000 kindergarten teachers and 3000 primary school teachers participated in the study.

For most of the 6-year-olds studied, results suggested that the educational transition into school appeared not to pose considerable difficulties or dysfunctions. The general level of school readiness and maturity was evaluated as good: 50 per cent of children obtained average results in the sphere of cognitive development, while 80–90 per cent showed a high level of socio-emotional functioning. Significant findings included a correlation between the level of cognitive development and the kind of educational institution attended by the children – the children who attended preschool settings had a higher level of cognitive maturity than children who attended kindergarten. Socio-emotional development was associated with gender – girls had higher levels of functioning than boys, entering new social roles with more ease and achieving better effectiveness in task situations.

Following the commencement of the reforms in the 2009/2010 school year, a comparative analysis (Kienig 2011) was made of the socio-emotional functioning of 6-year-old children in three settings: preschool; kindergarten at a primary school; and the first year of primary school. At the end of the first school year of the reform, the study involved 60 children (36 girls and 24 boys) aged 6 years 4 months to 7 years 5 months. Twenty children attended a kindergarten group (11 girls and 9 boys), 20 children attended a kindergarten department at a primary school (10 girls and 10 boys) and 20 children (15 girls and 5 boys) attended first grade in five Bialystok primary schools. Due to the low number of 6-year-old children who began school in 2009/2010 and to those children attending different schools, the schools did not open separate classes for their 6-year-olds and they were included in first grade with 7-year-olds.

The data included an assessment of children's social adjustment at school using Schaefer and Aaronson's Classroom Behaviour Inventory Preschool to Primary Scale (CBI) (Schaefer, Aaronson & Burgon 1968) based on observations of children's behaviour by parents and teachers.

Children's socio-emotional functioning

The results from the CBI show differences in the level of socio-emotional functioning among the 6-year-old children from the different types of institutions. The 6-year-old children attending preschool groups achieved the lowest results in the area of general functioning. These results contradict the opinion that it is the preschool setting that creates the best situation for development of children's social and emotional competences as compared with the kindergarten in primary school and a first-year primary school classroom. What seems especially interesting is that the children attending the kindergarten achieved better results in comparison not only with preschool children but also with those attending first grade, and includes the dimension of the CBI that assesses behaviours aimed at executing tasks, including those typical for schoolwork. However, when results were differentiated for gender, results indicated that girls had higher levels of social competence than boys and showed greater adaptability to new situations. Given that there were three times as many girls (*n*=15) as boys in the sub-group of participants in the study who were in Grade 1, it is likely that the findings showing more positive outcomes for children who had commenced school are more reflective of gender than school effects.

Parents and teachers of 6-year-old children from preschool settings, kindergarten and first grade were asked to rate their children as high functioning in the following areas: social and emotional well-being, positive relationship with peers, social independence, cooperation with peers, problem-solving skills, coping with stress. Responses by parents and teachers in relation to the different areas of social and emotional competences of children showed that a high level of social and emotional skills was evident in only about 30 per cent of the children taking part in the research.

There were differences in the assessment of children's functioning depending on the aspect of competence as well as what institution the child attended. In the opinion of both their parents and teachers, 6-year-olds from all educational environments displayed a high level of well-being (contentment and positive emotions connected to being in kindergarten/school), had positive relationships with peers and the ability to cope with difficult situations. On the other hand, what was shown to pose the most difficulty for the children was self-reliance and dealing with negative emotions.

Differences in the opinions of parents and teachers were also noted. Parents, more often than teachers, identified with the children's high level of the sense of well-being, their ability to cooperate with peers and their self-reliance (only the children from preschool and kindergarten). Teachers, more often than parents, noted positive relations between the children and their peers, and their ability to cope with challenges. These differences in opinion reflect the different perspectives of parents and teachers not only about a child but also observations of children's behaviour in different social contexts. The most congruent opinions concerning children's functioning occurred for teachers and parents of children attending the preschool setting, which results from close and long-lasting mutual relations, enabling an exchange of opinions on the child's behaviour. The differences shown between parents' and teachers' assessment of children who attended kindergarten and first grade may be related to more limited relationships due to children only being in those settings for one year and the fewer opportunities for sharing information on the children's functioning.

Discussion

Studies in Britain (Fabian 2002), Germany (Griebel & Niesel 2002) and Australia (Margetts 2002a) have emphasised the importance of social and emotional skills for an auspicious school start. A sense of emotional well-being is found to be especially helpful to children faced with new social situations (Broström 2002; Bulkeley & Fabian 2006; Griebel & Niesel 2002). In the current study, only 30 per cent of children were rated as having high levels of social and emotional competence, and this was greater for girls than for boys, and for children in school settings. Given that 6-year-old children who attended kindergarten had the lowest overall socio-emotional competence and that kindergarten departments in schools may provide benefits for the development of these skills, further research should investigate the practices of teachers in the different settings in which 6-year-olds participate in order to identify possible reasons for these differences.

Given the differences in the ratings of parents and teachers, the results obtained do not give an unequivocal answer to the question of whether 6-year-old children really do cope better in kindergarten or school – the kind of institution may not be so important, but rather it may be more vital to focus the attention of both parents and teachers of children of kindergarten age on stimulating their development in various spheres, including the socio-emotional sphere. As noted by Broström (2002) and Dunlop (2002), children's coping with school is supported when there is communication between all the people and cooperation between schools and kindergartens in sharing information about children and building curricular continuity and co-constructing transition activities.

Special attention should be paid to the children who experience difficulties in educational transition into their first grade of primary school. Based on the work of Kienig, this includes giving particular attention to the development of social and emotional competencies in boys.

It is necessary that we undertake further, more detailed studies examining the functioning of 6-year-olds at school and, simultaneously, create a platform for cooperation for all those interested in an auspicious start at school for children: the parents, the teachers and the researchers.

References

Bronfenbrenner, U. (1979) *The Ecology of Human Development: Experiments by Nature and Design*, Cambridge: Harvard University Press.

Broström, S. (2002) 'Communication and continuity in the transition from kindergarten to school', in H. Fabian and A.W. Dunlop (eds.) *Transitions in the Early Years: Debating Continuity and Progression for Children in Early Education*, London: RoutledgeFalmer.

Brzezińska, A.I. (2005) *Psychologiczne Portrety Człowieka*, Gdańsk: GWP.

Brzezińska, A. and Czub, T. (1991) 'Trudności w adaptacji do nowego środowiska – trudności wychowawcze', *Wychowanie w Przedszkolu* 2: 261–270.

Brzezińska, A., Appelt, K. and Ziółkowska, B. (2008) 'Psychologia rozwoju człowieka', in J. Strelau and D. Doliński (eds.) *Psychologia. Podręcznik Akademicki*, Vol. 2, Gdańsk: GWP.

Brzezińska, A.I., Matejczuk, J. and Nowotnik, A. (2012) 'Wspomaganie rozwoju dzieci w wieku od 5 do 7 lat a ich gotowość do radzenia sobie z wyzwaniami szkoły', *Edukacja* 1(117): 7–22.

Bulkeley, J. and Fabian, H. (2006) 'Well-being and belonging during early educational transitions', *International Journal of Transitions in Childhood* 2: 18–30.

Denham, S. (1998) *Emotional Development in Young Children*, New York: Guilford Press.

Dockett, S. and Perry, B. (2007) *Transitions to School: Perceptions, Expectations, Experiences*, Sydney: UNSW Press.

Dunlop, A.W. (2002) *Early Years Educational Transitions: Study for Stirling Council*, Glasgow: University of Strathclyde/Stirling Council.

Einarsdottir, J. (2003) 'When the bell rings we have to go inside: Preschool children's views on the primary school', *European Early Childhood Educational Research Journal. Transitions, Themed Monograph Series* 1: 35–50.

Fabian, H. (2002) 'Empowering children for transitions', in H. Fabian and A.W. Dunlop (eds.) *Transitions in the Early Years* (pp. 123–134), London: RoutledgeFalmer.

Fabian, H. and Dunlop, A.W. (eds.) (2002) *Transitions in the Early Years: Debating Continuity and Progression for Children in Early Education*, London: RoutledgeFalmer.

Fabian, H. and Dunlop, A.W. (2005) 'The importance of play in transitions', in J.R. Moyles (ed.) *The Excellence of Play* (2nd edn.), Berkshire: Open University Press/McGraw-Hill.

Fabian, H. and Dunlop, A.W. (2006) 'Outcomes of good practice in transition processes for children entering primary school'. Paper commissioned for the Education for All Global Monitoring Report 2007, *Strong Foundations: Early Childhood Care and Education*. Online, available at: <http://unesdoc.unesco.org/images/0014/001474/147463e.pdf> (accessed June 2012).

Griebel, W. and Niesel, R. (2002) 'Co-constructing transition into kindergarten and school by children, parents and teachers', in H. Fabian and A.W. Dunlop (eds.) *Transitions in the Early Years* (pp. 64–75), London: RoutledgeFalmer.

Griebel, W. and Niesel, R. (2003) 'Successful transitions: Social competencies help pave the way into kindergarten and school', *European Early Childhood Education Research Monograph* 1: 25–33.

Griebel, W. and Niesel, R. (2005) 'Transition competence and resiliency in educational institutions', *International Journal of Transitions in Childhood* 1: 4–11.

Halberstadt, A.G., Dunsmore, J.C. and Denham, S.A. (2001) 'Affective social competence', *Social Development* 10: 79–119.

Havighurst, R.J. (1972) *Developmental Tasks and Education*, New York: David McKay.

Hubbart, J.A. and Coie, J.D. (1994) 'Emotional correlates of social competence in children's peer relationships', *Merrill-Palmer Quarterly* 40: 1–20.

Jaszczyszyn, E. (2010) *Oczekiwania sześciolatków i ich rodziców w stosunku do szkoły a realia realizacji obowiązku szkolnego*, Białystok: Trans-Humana.

Kielar-Turska, M. (2011) 'Średnie dzieciństwo – wiek przedszkolny', in J. Trempała (ed.) *Psychologia Rozwoju Człowieka*, Warszawa: Wydawnictwo Naukowe PWN.

Kienig, A. (2005) 'Funkcjonowanie społeczne małego dziecka w nowym środowisku', in S. Guz and J. Andrzejewska (eds.) *Wybrane Problemy Edukacji Dzieci w Przedszkolu i Szkole* (pp. 245–251), Lublin: Wyd. UMCS.

Kienig, A. (2011) 'Sześciolatek w szkole. społeczno-emocjonalne wymiary przejścia edukacyjnego', *Edukacja* 3(115): 50–56.

Kopik, A. (ed.) (2007) *Sześciolatki w Polsce. Raport 2006. Diagnoza badanych sfer rozwoju*, Kielce: Akademia Świetokrzyska.

Margetts, K. (2002a) 'Planning transition programmes', in H. Fabian and A.W. Dunlop (eds.) *Transitions in the Early Years* (pp. 111–122), London: RoutledgeFalmer.

Margetts, K. (2002b) 'Transition to school – complexity and diversity', *European Early Childhood Education Research Journal* 10(2): 103–114.

Murawska, B. (2004) *Segregacja na progu szkoły podstawowej*, Warszawa: Instytut Spraw Publicznych.

Schaefer, E.S., Aaronson, M.R. and Burgon, B.R. (1968) *Classroom Behavior Inventory*, Chicago, IL: National Institute of Mental Health.

Schaffer, H.R. (2005) *Psychologia Dziecka*, Warszawa: PWN.

Schaffer, H.R. (2010) *Psychologia Rozwojowa. Podstawowe Pojęcia*, Kraków: Wydawnictwo Uniwersytetu Jagiellońskiego.

Sikorska, J. (2008) 'Wiedza dzieci 6-letnich o szkole', *Przegląd Badań Edukacyjnych* 1(6): 73–82.

Stefańska-Klar, R. (2000) 'Późne dzieciństwo. Młodszy wiek szkolny', in B. Harwas-Napierała and J. Trempała (eds.) *Psychologia rozwoju człowieka. Charakterystyka o kresów życia człowiek* (pp. 130–162), Warszawa: PWN.

Sowińska, H. (ed.) (2011) *Dziecko w szkolnej rzeczywistości. Założonya rzeczywisty obraz edukacji elementarnej*, Poznań: Wyd. Naukowe UAM.

Szlendak, T. (2003) *Zaniedbanapiaskownica*. Warszawa: Instytut Spraw Publicznych.

4

INCLUSION AND TRANSITION TO SCHOOL IN AUSTRALIA

Anne Petriwskyj

Policies of educational inclusion in Australia have challenged traditional notions of children's school readiness and the practice of grade retention. Teachers confront competing demands for inclusion of diverse learners and for meeting national statutory assessment pressures in schools. Policy initiatives such as changes to the school entry age, improvements to early education and development of national curriculum documents have aimed to support transition to school, yet have proved insufficient to cater for the diversity of school entrants. Teachers are exploring transition pedagogies that maintain continuity of learning between home, community, early childhood programmes and school. Changes in education both before school and within schools are emerging to address competing demands and varied notions of transition to school.

Introduction: Transitions in Australia

Historically, school entry has been framed by emphasis on the academic and socio-emotional readiness of individual children for a school environment, and on the responsibilities of families and teachers prior to school. Recent international literature has highlighted the impact of the ready school and of transition processes shared between early childhood services, schools, families and communities, particularly for children with diverse abilities and sociocultural backgrounds (Dockett & Perry 2009; Dunlop & Fabian 2007; Graue 2006). More inclusive processes and improved coordination between sending programmes (e.g. preschools) and receiving programmes (e.g. schools) are indicated.

While all stakeholders are important to transition, teachers are a significant variable in efforts to improve educational processes (Lingard & Mills 2003). They have immediate responsibility for implementation of transition policy, for pedagogic decision-making and for maintenance of professional networks and family–community partnerships impacting on transition to school. This chapter will, therefore, focus on teachers in the early years of school and in early childhood education and care (ECEC) before school in the current Australian context.

Impact on transition of teacher beliefs

The underlying beliefs that teachers hold about transition and diversity frame their practices in ways that can unintentionally marginalise groups of children. Those teachers who believe that children should be ready for the academic or socio-emotional demands of the school environment have been reticent to support school entry for immature children (Petriwskyj 2010). In a study of transition for children with disabilities, Walker and colleagues (2012) found that teachers who identified significant transition difficulties were more likely to rate regular class inclusion as inappropriate because of readiness concerns.

Differences in beliefs between teachers in ECEC programmes and the early years of school provide a context for discontinuities during transition. Timperley et al. (2003) found that discontinuities in the approaches to transition of teachers in ECEC and school were based on differing beliefs about quality teaching and the meaning of transition. The transition focus has been on the shift from play-based to outcomes-based curricula involving ECEC to school classes (Bablett et al. 2011) or the first year of school to Grade 1 (O'Gorman 2008; Petriwskyj 2010), depending on the school system in each Australian state. Thus the contextual circumstances surrounding transition decision-making, as well as teacher beliefs, require consideration.

Impact on transition of competing pressures

Australian ECEC and schools are expected to make changes to provide high quality education for all children, regardless of ability or background (Department of Education, Employment and Workplace Relations (DEEWR) 2009; MCEECDYA 2008). Alongside these expectations of inclusion, teachers confront demands to improve educational outcomes, particularly for target groups (e.g. indigenous children) identified in the Melbourne Declaration on Educational Goals for Young Australians (MCEECDYA 2008). This tension between inclusive policies and normative outcome expectations has impacted on transitions by broadening the time frame and approaches to transition.

The competing demands to include a wide range of children and meet national statutory assessment requirements supported an initial emphasis on ECEC quality and preparation for school entry. In some states, formal readiness assessment was undertaken (Boardman 2006) although such assessment has been criticised for a deficit focus and for cultural inappropriateness, particularly for indigenous children (McTurk et al. 2011). The national Australian Early

Development Index (AEDI) aims to identify community disadvantage in order to direct resources to community support for readiness rather than to individual children, yet its use is potentially stigmatising (Agbenyega 2009). Criticism that this emphasis on children's readiness prioritises normative development over inclusive provision for diversity has led to reframing of the debate around the ready school and shared preparedness, in line with recent international trends (Dunlop & Fabian 2007; Graue 2006).

Preparedness for school entry

Teachers and parents who understand transition as a single school-entry change event maintain a focus on preparation prior to school (O'Gorman 2008; Petriwskyj 2010). Preparation includes school orientation visits, attention to children's social skills, a staggered start to school and more academically oriented teaching towards the end of ECEC (Bablett et al. 2011; Dockett & Perry 2009). Awareness that preparedness also involves parents and other teachers has extended orientation programmes to include meetings with parents and links between teachers to discuss transition (Victorian Department of Education and Early Childhood Development (DEECD) 2010). While preparation supports a shared sense of confidence at school entry, it does not address the complexity of early years school classes, children's personal resources and individual factors influencing transitions.

The ready school and shared preparedness

Attention has been drawn to the need for schools to change in order to cater for diverse class groups (DEECD 2010). Processes of transition to school in an inclusive context imply adjustments that schools need to make for the reality of diversity in classrooms. Australian research has considered the separate concerns of gender, disability, cultural and linguistic experience, indigenous background, rural location, geographic mobility, social and economic circumstances, giftedness and refugee experience (Boardman 2006; Henderson 2004; Jackson 2006; MacDonald 2008; McTurk et al. 2011; Raban & Ure 2000; Whitton 2005) as well as the overarching concerns of inclusive schools (Petriwskyj 2010). This evidence on transition indicates that it is a complex process, involving a range of people and settings, and that schools need to prepare for the diversity of school entrants.

One key shift has been the emphasis on shared responsibility for transition, including the role of schools as well as ECEC centres, in ensuring continuity in children's education. Partnerships of schools with families and communities offer opportunities for shared preparedness and a sense of confidence (Ashton et al. 2008; McTurk et al. 2011; Thorpe et al. 2005). Shared transition processes in an inclusive context support children, families and communities while ensuring that those facing challenges are not stigmatised. Policy, pedagogy and systems initiatives seek to address new expectations of shared preparedness.

Policy initiatives to support transition

Policy changes in Australia to support transition include both short-term strategies focused on adjustment during school entry, and longer-term approaches sustaining children's progress before and within school.

Policy on school entry age

Older age of school entry has been found in Australia to assist transition to school for boys in particular (Boardman 2006), although this conflicts with international evidence that children from challenging home environments progress more quickly if school entry is not delayed (Stipek 2002). The eligible age of entry to the first year of schooling (the year before Grade 1) in Australian schools is 4½ to 5 years (Dockett & Perry 2009) and children must commence school by 6 years of age (compulsory starting age). However, variations by state jurisdiction remain (e.g. the year before Grade 1 is compulsory in only some states), creating challenges for geographically mobile children.

Since concerns remain about the capacity of some children to commence school at the typical age, policy variations to the age of entry include delayed entry of children with disabilities and accelerated entry of gifted children (e.g. Education Queensland 2007). However, the structure, quality and coherence of educational programmes, rather than the timing of school entry, may be key factors.

Policy on access to quality early childhood programmes

Evidence that children's background of experience is the major influence in school success has promoted the increasing provision of universally accessible ECEC programmes (Bowes et al. 2009; DEEWR 2008). Wider provision of high quality ECEC has included quality improvement processes and government funding of part-time preschool education (DEEWR 2008). Concern for equitable access to ECEC for rural, socially marginalised and indigenous children has been addressed through targeted funding of programmes for these groups (DEEWR 2008). Debate about the quality of ECEC programmes, and about whether they offer sufficient opportunity to adjust to the expectations of schools (Bowes et al. 2009), has prompted national curriculum initiatives and professional learning programmes for ECEC teachers.

Early years education initiatives

Early childhood national curriculum documents have been developed in Australia for ECEC, and have been used in one state for programmes across the birth to 8-year age range (DEECD 2010). Alignment between ECEC and the early years of school has been partially addressed in the national Early Years

Learning Framework for ECEC (DEEWR 2009) and the Australian Curriculum for schools (Australian Curriculum, Assessment and Reporting Authority (ACARA) 2010) through the shared use of learning outcomes, yet discrepancies between these curricula impact on transition to school. The ECEC framework emphasises social inclusion, holistic outcomes and continuity during transition to school, while the school curriculum emphasises academic subject content outcomes (ACARA 2010). Thus national curricula address transitions across the nation's education systems (e.g. for children who are geographically mobile), yet do not account as effectively for transition into school.

While these policy changes represent significant efforts to address social inequity and improve outcomes, they are insufficient to cater for the complexity of contemporary school classrooms (Thorpe et al. 2005). This requires pedagogic as well as policy changes to take diverse transition factors into consideration.

Pedagogic initiatives to support transition

Pedagogic changes supporting transition to school are informed by an emerging awareness of the role of continuity, relationships and children's competency (Petriwskyj, Thorpe & Tayler 2005), and a shift in early education towards sociocultural and critical theories (Grieshaber 2009).

Continuity of experience between ECEC and school

Continuity between year levels of education offers children opportunities to maintain progress without the shock of abrupt change (Greishaber 2009). One strategy has been to make ECEC programmes more school-like, particularly towards the end of the preschool year, to introduce children to the culture and style of formal schooling (Petriwskyj 2005b). Carefully focused play-based learning in the early years of school has also been found to smooth transition, concurring with international evidence (Broström 2005; Petriwskyj 2010). Pedagogic discontinuities between ECEC and school classes indicate that teachers need to be aware of the theories that underpin their practice and that of colleagues, in order to engage in fruitful debate about transition continuity (Grieshaber 2009). It may also be necessary to improve resourcing for early years school classes (e.g. classroom equipment, teacher–child ratios) to offer better continuity of experience for children (Petriwskyj 2005a).

Teacher communication and programme continuity

Communication links between teachers at various year levels offer opportunities to enhance the continuity of children's learning. Teachers may share child assessment information, discuss strategies for teaching individuals, identify child groupings that may be successful in planning classes and visit one another's classes (Petriwskyj et al. 2005). However, reliance on such connections assumes that children have access to linked programmes, remain enrolled in one place and attend regularly. These strategies may not be sufficient for children who are frequently hospitalised, for children with complex circumstances and for geographically mobile children whose education is disrupted (Dockett et al. 2011; Henderson 2004; Shiu 2004). They may also not take into account limited preschool access in rural areas, or for groups such as indigenous children or refugees who may utilise informal playgroups or no ECEC programmes (Jackson 2006; MacDonald 2008; McTurk et al. 2011). Sustained quality of education is problematic for gifted children, for whom transition processes offering continuity in learning are often overlooked (Whitton 2005). Specialist educational support for children with disabilities also needs to be sustained if their progress is to continue (Walker et al. 2012). More complex strategies, incorporating home/community–school links and system coordination, are required to ensure continuity for children with a range of abilities and backgrounds.

Continuity between home/community and school

Continuity between home/community and school, as well as between year levels of education, offers children the security of congruence between what they already know and what they are learning (Ashton et al. 2008). Such continuity is of particular importance for children from culturally and linguistically diverse backgrounds, facing a confusing clash of expectations as they commence school (McTurk et al. 2011; Sanagavarapu 2010). This presents a particular challenge to children who have attended no ECEC programme prior to school entry, such as some indigenous children (McTurk et al. 2011). Contrasts between home and school have also been identified as a challenge for children from socially and economically diverse backgrounds, particularly those living in extreme poverty (Dockett et al. 2011; Raban & Ure 2000). Thorpe and colleagues (2005) found that school teachers' recognition of difference and incorporation of cultural knowledge was low. Teachers reported relying on cultural teaching assistants, where these were available, for information on language and culturally appropriate practices (Petriwskyj 2010). Professional learning for teachers in cultural diversity could assist in forming more productive relationships with diverse families and communities in order to support transitions.

Relationships that support transitions

Supportive relationships ease the pressures of transition for children who feel insecure and enhance all children's sense of belonging (Bablett et al. 2011; Bowes et al. 2009; Grieshaber 2009). These relationships include child friendships or other peer interactions, teacher–child interactions and teacher–family partnerships. Teachers have tended to focus on internal relationships within the school (e.g. buddy programmes, multi-age social learning groups) to build supportive relationships that enhance smooth transition to school (Dockett et al. 2011; Petriwskyj 2010). However, teachers in schools have given more limited attention to external relationships with ECEC services, families and communities that have been identified as a key support for transitions, particularly in socially and culturally diverse communities (Ashton et al. 2008; McTurk et al. 2011; Thorpe et al. 2005). Family–community consultation and transition networks offer opportunities for all stakeholders to share in the design of transition strategies that suit the local community circumstances (DEECD 2010; Thorpe et al. 2005).

Reduction in contact between teachers and families as children enter school limits the development of productive home–community–school partnerships (Ashton et al. 2008), which is of particular concern for families in low socio-economic circumstances, indigenous families and families of children with disabilities (Grieshaber 2009; Walker et al. 2012). While Raban and Ure (2000) found that teachers of socially and economically diverse children viewed transition difficulties as lack of readiness, parents reported that rigid school expectations, child boredom and frequent changes of teacher contributed to these difficulties. Lack of family consultation and low expectations have limited opportunities for teachers of indigenous children to build upon strengths such as resilience and extended family support (McTurk et al. 2011). Australian Bangladeshi and Korean families have expressed concern that children's school adjustment was hampered not only by limited English proficiency, but also by school expectations that contrasted with home socialisation practices (Millar 2011; Sanagavarapu 2010). These tensions indicate a lack of cultural understanding and a construction of sociocultural diversity as deficit. Such constructions are not aligned with current understandings of inclusion in Australia, and could inhibit effective transition. Broader reforms within school education as well as in ECEC are indicated to enhance inclusion and transitions.

System-level and whole-school reforms

Reforms within education systems to improve inclusion and align ECEC and school settings offer opportunities for a more seamless transition process. System-level reforms to enhance transition include combining ECEC and school within a single government department, establishing transition policy and coordinating support service delivery (DEECD 2010). Continuity of support service provision as children enter school is an important consideration for those accessing services for English as a second language or for disability (Dockett et al. 2011; Walker et al. 2012). While transition plans enhance continuity of services and learning, their enactment may require a transition coordinator to clarify roles and processes (Dockett et al. 2011; Queensland Studies Authority 2010).

Teachers in the early years of school have identified school-level support for classroom initiatives as a crucial component of transforming transition processes

(Petriwskyj 2005a). Whole-school approaches that support transitions include shared professional learning programmes for teachers, collaborative decision-making and multi-age social learning programmes for children. Learning support teachers and teaching assistants, as well as classroom teachers, have a role in enacting inclusive transition processes (Petriwskyj 2010). School playground supervisors' roles also require attention in transition planning because of the psychosocial issues arising in less adult-controlled settings (Petriwskyj 2005b). However, the leadership demonstrated by school principals is vital to whole-school coordination and family–community collaboration directed towards ensuring coherent and inclusive transition processes (Thorpe et al. 2005).

Conclusion

Although traditional notions of children's readiness for school have been reinterpreted in contemporary Australia as a focus on preparation for school, broader transition processes take the diversity of the population and inclusive policies into account. Evolving inclusive transition processes involve both structural and pedagogic changes to address the diverse range of abilities and backgrounds in school entrants, in line with international trends. While policy provisions both before and within schools provide a frame for more consistent access to and quality of early education, pedagogic changes and whole-school processes attend to the diversity of school entrants. Attention to longer-term strategies, clearer policy settings, systemic educational change, relationships with families and communities and professional learning in teachers form a broader approach to transition processes that are more inclusive and effective.

References

Agbenyega, J. (2009) 'The Australian Early Development Index: Who does it measure: Piaget or Vygotsky's child?', *Australian Journal of Early Childhood* 34: 31–38.

Ashton, J., Woodrow, C., Johnston, C., Wangamann, J., Singh, L. and James, T. (2008) 'Partnerships in learning: Linking early childhood services, families and schools for optimal development', *Australasian Journal of Early Childhood* 33: 10–16.

Australian Curriculum, Assessment and Reporting Authority (ACARA) (2010) *Draft Australian Curriculum*. Online, available at: <http://www.australiancurriculum.edu.au/guide> (accessed May 2012).

Bablett, L., Barratt-Pugh, C., Kilgallon, P. and Maloney, C. (2011) 'Transition from long day care to kindergarten: Continuity or not?' *Australasian Journal of Early Childhood* 36: 42–49.

Boardman, M. (2006) 'The impact of age and gender on prep children's academic achievements', *Australian Journal of Early Childhood* 31: 1–6.

Bowes, J., Harrison. L., Sweller, N., Taylor, A. and Neilsen-Hewett, C. (2009) 'From childcare to school: Influences on children's adjustment and achievement in the year before school and in the first year of school'. Report to New South Wales Department of Community Services, July 2009.

Broström, S. (2005) 'Transition problems and play as a transitory activity', *Australian Journal of Early Childhood* 30: 17–26.

Department of Education, Employment and Workplace Relations (DEEWR) (2008) *Early Childhood Education: Universal Access*. Online, available at: <http://www.deewr. gov.au/EarlyChildhoodPolicy_Agenda?ECUA/Pages/home.aspx> (accessed May 2012).

Department of Education, Employment and Workplace Relations (DEEWR) (2009) *Belonging, Being and Becoming: The Early Years Learning Framework for Australia*, Canberra: Commonwealth of Australia.

Dockett, S. and Perry, B. (2009) 'Readiness for school: A relational construct', *Australasian Journal of Early Childhood* 34: 20–26.

Dockett, S., Perry, B., Kearney, E., Hampshire, A., Mason, J. and Schmied, V. (2011) *Facilitating Children's Transition to School from Families with Complex Support Needs*, Albury: Research Institute for Professional Practice, Learning and Education, Charles Sturt University. Online, available at: <http://www.csu.edu.au/research/ripple/ publications/index.htm> (accessed May 2012).

Dunlop, A.W. and Fabian, H. (2007) *Informing Transitions in the Early Years: Research, Policy and Practice*, Maidenhead: McGraw-Hill.

Education Queensland (2007) *Variation to School Age Entry Enrolment*. Online, available at:<http://www.education.qld.gov.au/strategic/eppr/students/smspr007> (accessed May 2012).

Graue, B. (2006) 'The answer is readiness – now what is the question?' *Early Education and Development* 17: 43–56.

Grieshaber, S. (2009) 'Equity and quality in the early years of schooling', *Curriculum Perspective* 29: 91–97.

Henderson, R. (2004) 'Educational issues for the children of itinerant seasonal farm workers: A case study in an Australian context', *International Journal of Inclusive Education* 8: 293–310.

Jackson, D. (2006) 'Playgroups as protective environments for refugee children at risk of trauma', *Australian Journal of Early Childhood* 31: 1–5.

Lingard, B. and Mills, M. (2003) 'Teachers' and school reform: Working with productive pedagogies and productive assessment', *Melbourne Studies in Education* 42: 1–18.

MacDonald, A. (2008) 'Kindergarten transition in a small rural school: From planning to implementation', *Education in Rural Australia* 18: 13–21.

MCEECDYA (2008) *Melbourne Declaration on Educational Goals for Young Australians*. Online, available at: <http://www.mceecdya.edu.au/verve/_resources/National_ Declaration_on_the_Educational_Goals_for_Young_Australians.pdf> (accessed May 2012).

McTurk. N., Lea, T., Robinson, G., Nutton, G. and Carapetis, J. (2011) 'Defining and assessing the school readiness of Indigenous Australian children', *Australasian Journal of Early Childhood* 36: 69–76.

Millar, N. (2011) 'Korean children's cultural adjustment during transition to the early years of school in Australia', *Australasian Journal of Early Childhood* 36: 10–17.

O'Gorman, L. (2008) 'The preparatory year in a Queensland non-government school: Exploring parents' views', *Australian Journal of Early Childhood* 33: 51–58.

Petriwskyj, A. (2005a) 'Pedagogical issues in transition to school', in J-B. Son and S. O'Neill (eds.) *Enhancing Learning and Teaching: Pedagogies of Technology and Language*, Flaxton: Post Pressed.

Petriwskyj, A. (2005b) 'Transition to school: Early years teachers' roles', *Australian Research in Early Childhood Education* 12: 39–50.

Petriwskyj, A. (2010) 'Diversity and inclusion in the early years', *International Journal of Inclusive Education* 14: 195–212.

Petriwskyj, A., Thorpe, K. and Tayler, C. (2005) 'Trends in construction of transition to school in three western regions 1999–2004', *International Journal of Early Years Education* 13: 55–69.

Queensland Studies Authority (2010) *Queensland Kindergarten Learning Guideline*. Online, available at: <http://www.qsa.qld.edu.au/10192.html> (accessed May 2012).

Raban, B. and Ure, C. (2000) 'Continuity for socially disadvantaged school entrants: Perspectives of parents and teachers', *Australian Research in Early Childhood Education* 7: 54–65.

Sanagavarapu, P. (2010) 'Children's transition to school: Voices of Bangladeshi parents in Sydney, Australia', *Australasian Journal of Early Childhood* 35: 21–29.

Shiu, S. (2004) 'Maintaining the thread: Including young children with chronic illness in the primary classroom', *Australian Journal of Early Childhood* 29: 33–38.

Stipek, D. (2002) 'At what age should children enter kindergarten? A question for policymakers and parents', *Social Policy Report* 16: 3–16.

Thorpe, K., Tayler, C., Bridgstock, R., Grieshaber, S., Skoien, P., Danby, S. and Petriwskyj, A. (2005) *Preparing for School: Report of the Queensland Preparing for School Trials*, Brisbane: Queensland University of Technology & Department of Education and Training.

Timperley, H., McNaughton, S., Howie, L. and Robinson, V. (2003) 'Transitioning children from early childhood education to school: Teachers' beliefs and transition practices', *Australian Journal of Early Childhood* 28: 32–38.

Victorian Department of Education and Early Childhood Development (DEECD) (2010) *Transition: A Positive Start to School Resource Kit*. Online, available at: <www.education.vic.gov.au/earlylearning> (accessed May 2012).

Walker, S., Nicholson, S., Carrington, S., Dunbar, S., Hand, K., Whiteford, C., Meldrum, K. and Berthelsen, D. (2012) 'The transition to school of children with developmental disabilities: Views of parents and teachers', *Australasian Journal of Early Childhood* 37: 22–29.

Whitton, D. (2005) 'Transition to school for gifted children', *Australian Journal of Early Childhood* 30: 27–31.

PART III

Outcomes for children and children's perspectives

5

TOWARDS SUCCESSFUL TRANSITIONS

Hilary Fabian

This chapter addresses questions concerning the way in which children can be supported to achieve positive transitions. It is based on well-established theory and draws together relevant practice, raising questions that can help practitioners to consider their current procedures for children starting school. It begins by highlighting some transition challenges and goes on to explore how successful transitions might be achieved through the domains of learning, sociocultural understanding, emotional well-being and communication. The key outcomes are that curriculum continuity requires policies that support liaison between settings; friendships ease the anxiety of new situations; resilience and confidence contribute to children's sense of being in control of the transition; and co-constructing the transition programme clarifies the learning process.

Overview: Transition to school in England and Wales

Transition and change are part of everyone's experience but to recognise and understand their impact they must be seen in the context of a child's life (Department for Education and Science 2003). Getting the transition to school right is important because, if it goes wrong, there can be long-lasting and far-reaching consequences such as social and emotional difficulties, which can cause educational problems (Margetts 2002). In addition at this time, there are much greater levels of independence, responsibility and self-regulation expected of children than previously (Dockett & Perry 2007), which might also lead to problems with well-being. So how are all those involved with the transition to school able to help each child develop sociocultural understanding, achieve emotional well-being and maximise their learning without interruption? This chapter addresses this question by outlining links between theories and practice through themes that can frame and support the transition process to school.

In England and Wales children can attend some form of state or privately funded early childcare provision from birth to 5 years of age. Until the age of 5 they follow a play-based curriculum, Foundation Stage 1, which takes place in a childcare setting such as a nursery between the ages of 3 and 4, but it is non-compulsory education. Foundation Stage 2 takes place in the Reception class of a school between the ages of 4 and 5 years. Children then begin a more formal curriculum, Key Stage 1, which is the legal term for the two years of schooling in maintained schools in England and Wales normally known as Year 1 and Year 2, when pupils are aged between 5 and 7. Although children do not have to attend school until the beginning of the term following their fifth birthday, most local authorities have a policy of accepting children into school at the beginning of the term during which they become 5. Therefore the physical move to 'big school' usually takes place when children start in the Reception class.

Challenges of transition

The move from home and childcare to school involves coping with physical, social and philosophical differences. As children grapple for success they must make sense of the differences, develop resilience – the ability to adjust to change – and overcome any obstacles to their learning. In seeking the 'reality' of the new situation children must interpret their physical environment and the explicit rules that govern their behaviour within it – the way they dress, the language that is used, significant activities and so on. This new reality is also characterised by assumptions about social understandings – the role of groups, classroom values, the accepted way to interact and the significance of particular aspects of the day (Fabian 2007). So the challenge for children is not only to understand the differences and essentials of the beliefs and systems of home/childcare with the events and complex layers of the classroom, but also to integrate them to create a synergy (Campbell Clark 2000).

Challenges for educators involve understanding the range of expectations and perspectives of others, including children, to achieve curriculum continuity and socio-emotional well-being in the new setting. They need to see transition as schools and settings working together to mediate any discontinuities (Brooker 2008) rather than in terms of 'readiness' or 'adjustment'.

Usually it is the family who help children to negotiate the border between home/childcare and school. They play an important role in their child's ability to manage the different settings as they act as a bridge between the systems and affect the way the transition process is experienced (Griebel & Niesel 2002; Johansson 2002). However, some parents face emotional turmoil because once their child is in school they have to put their trust in the teachers to provide for their child's well-being, health and progress. On the other hand, this first major educational transition can be viewed as an opportunity for families and the education system to exchange information and work together to build children's dispositions to engage with change and develop resilience.

Successful transitions

Some children settle in quickly, whereas others take longer or experience difficulties, but successful transitions result in a child who feels strong, competent and able to handle new experiences with confidence. This involves children, families and settings working together to help children develop an understanding of change, which can lead to a virtuous cycle of transitions whereby children gain 'transitions capital' (Dunlop 2007: 164) resulting in cost-effectiveness in the long term. Ladd (2003: 3) suggests:

> A child can be seen as successful in school when she or he: (a) develops positive attitudes and feelings about school and learning, (b) establishes supportive social ties with teachers and classmates, (c) feels comfortable and relatively happy in the classroom rather than anxious, lonely or upset, (d) is interested and motivated to learn and take part in classroom activities (participation, engagement), and (e) achieves and progresses academically each school year.

This implies that physical, social and emotional well-being and learning are connected and that feeling 'suitable' (Broström 2002: 52) increases confidence to take part and learn. In addition, factors such as parents' and children's positive attitudes to school and to learning and teachers' expectations and methods of assessment will influence children's beliefs about themselves as learners, their self-esteem and their sense of identity. If these are right, then children are likely to have a sense of belonging to the school community and, as a result, succeed in their learning. Brooker (2008: 114–115) summarises a 'good' transition through themes such as a positive sense of identity, the presence of familiar adults and friends, understanding rules and routines, a sense of control and purpose and having an environment of opportunities.

In short, starting school requires the ability to have a sense of self, to be confident, to know what kind of behaviour is expected (and self-regulation to handle autonomy) and to get on with others. Furthermore, having a capacity to tolerate uncertainty, the ability to wait, the skill to follow directions and the capability to identify and ask for what you want are also advantages.

Continuity of learning

Underpinning much of the writing about transitions has been research that explores an ecological model (Bronfenbrenner 1979), cultural understanding (Bruner 1996), rites of passage (van Gennep 1960) and attachment (Bowlby 1988). However, in addition to these socio-emotional factors of becoming a pupil, children are expected to make progress with their learning. Curriculum progress across phases of education not only facilitates capable learners but also helps their confidence, thus improving their social and emotional well-being.

In early childhood settings children are active agents in their learning and are expected to negotiate their requirements. As children enter primary school education they have to adjust to a more adult-directed world in which decisions are made about what and when they will learn, and they encounter situations in which they are expected to be able to think in the abstract. Previous experiences influence the settling-in process, so similarities between systems in adjacent settings make it easier to integrate. Interconnectedness between settings comes about through shared responsibility and strong links at educational borders and cultural intersections (Peters 2010). For example, if children make visits to the new setting it is helpful if teachers have developed transition activities in conjunction with their early years colleagues that, in addition to ensuring children's well-being, reflect the way learning takes place in the school.

While children expect to make progress, the reality is sometimes different as they feel de-skilled and unable to manage time, resulting in 'dips' in their learning (Dunlop 2007: 164). Curriculum continuity can be supported by avoiding 'learning shocks' and building on children's achievements in small steps. Children can be helped to understand about learning at the next level through a supportive environment, through realising about being assessed and through knowing the structure of the school day. Having a good vocabulary is a main factor in successful learning. It is enhanced through the continuation of a play-based curriculum where children not only construct social knowledge and acquire an understanding of customs, but also stay motivated and interested in learning (Fabian & Dunlop 2005, 2010). Additionally, if classrooms are learning communities (Mayall 2007) where children work together collaboratively in a mutually respectful environment and then move forward together, they are likely to overcome any anxieties about learning.

To improve their understanding of curriculum continuity and provide appropriate learning on entry, staff bordering the transition can benefit from visiting one another and observing practice. By discussing 'cultural tools' such as children's drawings, scrapbooks and profile notes (Anning & Edwards 2006; Peters 2010), information about children's learning can be gained and their levels of attainment recognised. In addition to ensuring joined up working across settings and providing support for children's transition journeys, exchange visits can also give an insight into each other's teaching styles and perspectives of the way in which children learn.

For parents the 'seriousness of life' (Griebel & Niesel 2002: 70) begins at the start of full time education. If parents' expectations are to be fulfilled they need to realise that children usually begin school able to think and reason and with a desire to learn; that children are independent thinkers with the ability to make choices and with the mental flexibility to integrate formal and informal learning experiences. However, success at school also depends on children's abilities to interpret the teacher and understand the language of school. It is therefore helpful if the teacher can see situations from the child's point of view by gaining information from the parents in order to acknowledge and build on home learning, focus on children's strengths and recognise family expertise. This could come about by parents sharing examples of their child's learning with the teacher prior to starting school and the teacher providing an overview of a typical school day and outlining the way in which learning takes place at school.

In short, the move to school affords opportunities for children to see themselves as expert learners and successful people. However, supporting continuity of experiences for children requires policies and procedures that promote liaison between settings, the transfer of relevant information and the close involvement of parents and, where appropriate, other relevant professionals.

Social and cultural understanding

Starting school creates a change in relationships because the move from one setting to another has the potential for both making and breaking connections. The child's birth-year defines their cohort membership and, as a result, their relationships for several years, implying that *when* they live can result in a future where possible friendships – the might-have-beens – are lost. Certainly those children who start school with friends have an advantage (Brooker 2002; Hamre & Pianta 2001) as they provide a degree of security and a sense of continuity in the midst of change (Rutter & Rutter 1992). Therefore, to avoid a difficult start to new relationships, making and keeping friends should be supported. For example, by having photos of the class and asking each child to identify who they would like to play with during break can alleviate some of the anxieties that playtime can cause. The teacher's role is to enable meaningful interactions by 'tuning into' the way in which children experience their world and the influences beyond the school, to help them establish relationships both with their peers and adults. Helping children to make friends and be socially skilled means that they are more likely to have a succession of positive experiences and flourish in the new situation (Goleman 1996: 223). Planning for opportunities to make friends, for example, through group problem-based learning activities, can develop confidence to tackle new problems and an understanding of supporting and cooperating with one another.

During the first few months in the new situation children often spend time observing what is going on around them. Those joining established groups quickly adopt the behaviour of the class through watching accepted behaviours (Fabian 2002). Some schools take advantage of this by having a buddy system whereby children already in the class take on the role of mentor, teaching the social rules through everyday conversations and helping transitioners to make friends. As a result, levels of involvement increase and the proportion of time watching others reduces.

The social dimension or 'width-space' (Dencik 2006) during transitions is closely linked to the cultural dimension or 'depth-space' (Dencik 2006), expressed through the values, traditions and beliefs of the group. Each school has its own ethos so it is necessary to understand the local culture – the 'way of being' in a particular context – or 'neighbourhood effect' (Dockett & Perry 2007) if children are going to feel that they belong and have connectedness. To help children identify with the community and have this sense of togetherness, the cultural values of the setting must be made meaningful. Unfortunately, those who do not integrate or acquire the norms of the group often become marginalised, so encouraging individuals to participate in the life of the classroom is beneficial. Motivation to be part of the group is increased if children's own culture is acknowledged and if they are involved in co-constructing the group culture (Bruner 1996), for example, by showing their portfolio of previous learning to the class and talking about what is important to them. At the same time children are also cultivating their own identity by interacting and empathising with others in their social world.

In summary, cultural understanding and adaptive behaviour contribute to well-being as they give children greater confidence to ask questions, meet new expectations and take the initiative.

Emotional well-being

The terror of any new situation is in 'getting it wrong'. Children starting school are likely to have first day nerves about whether or not they will be liked, not knowing what to do, getting lost and so on. Indeed, siblings can sometimes peddle myths that may also cause stress. Some children are dealing with multiple or serial transitions such as moving house, changing country, joining a new family and so on. However, children can react very differently under the same conditions, depending on their level of resilience or 'capacity to bounce back' from adversity (Newman & Blackburn 2002). This results in them encountering either a painful transition or having an easy, enriching experience. Resilient children usually have social competence, problem-solving skills, autonomy and a sense of purpose and future (Krovetz 1999).

The question is how children maintain emotional well-being and a sense of self-identity when they move from a state of being confident, knowing everyone and where everything is, to one of not knowing in the new setting. Laevers et al. (1997) suggest that their emotional health is guaranteed if the situation meets their basic needs and they feel positive and involved. However, in order to achieve this state, children need feelings of initial success by being supported across the cultural border with threshold rites taking place in a neutral zone (van Gennep 1960: 18). These boundary areas between established systems are places in their own right (Peters 2010), where activities such as discussion are conducted about what they are looking forward to and areas of concern. Asking children about their expectations of the move to school allows adults to develop children's own ideas and support them to bridge their nursery and primary school experiences (Einarsdottir 2003). Listening to those involved in the transition process often produces surprises and has begun to add to current understandings of the way in which transition difficulties can be eased (Griebel & Niesel 2002).

Such discussions reveal that children may feel acutely embarrassed by their lack of knowledge or difficulty in finding their way around a new place, but also that they like their current abilities to be recognised (Dunlop 2007). Other 'border' activities include familiarisation tours that provide a window on the recognisable and the new, to build a picture of school, and mapping thoughts and feelings to identify emotions. These activities can cushion the move and develop competencies to assist the adaptation to school (Cefai 2008; Cowan & Hetherington 1991; Niesel & Griebel 2005). As a result, children are more likely to feel emotionally ready to meet the challenges of the new situation. Self-esteem and the child's emotional state are significant factors in being a successful learner (Ball 1994: 20), enabling a state of 'flow' where they are fully involved and absorbed in their learning (Csikszentmihalyi 1990).

At the start of school a child's emotional well-being can be further supported by the use of transitional objects (Campbell Clarke 2000) such as a family photograph or a special toy carried in the child's bag. Teachers can help by being sensitive to potential discontinuities, by providing visual prompts of routines and behaving 'as if' the child already has knowledge of the procedures (Edwards & Knight 1994: 14), in order to facilitate the classroom culture. A key aspect of emotional well-being is adult approval, which results in children feeling accepted as competent and worthwhile (Nutbrown 1996).

In summary, high levels of emotional well-being during transitions support children's self-confidence and enable them to be in control of the learning process. However, self-worth is not sufficient for success. Resilience gained from the support of family and activities in the boundary zone provide further protective factors.

Effective communication

Successful transition arrangements usually have sensitive and supportive communication structures running throughout them. By developing a culture of collaboration, informed practice can take place that bridges the gap between all those involved in the care and education of young children (Anning & Edwards 2006; Bronfenbrenner 1979). This co-construction of the transition is often developed through conversations about preparations for school and what happens at school (Niesel & Griebel 2007). The participants attempt to clarify how the processes of learning in different settings (home, early childhood setting and school) can be linked and optimised, following the principle that a child's knowledge and expertise should be valued, built on and developed at the beginning of formal schooling. When interacting with 'the other', there needs to be respect and a regard for differing values and beliefs in order for meanings to be understood by all parties. One way in which the co-construction can begin is by the family and early childhood educator visiting the school with photographs of the child both at home and in the early childhood setting. These can be used to introduce the teacher to the child's background. In addition the Profile report should inform a dialogue between Reception and Year 1 teachers about each child's stage of development and learning needs (Department for Education 2012: 11. para 2.8). Through listening to one another, information is shared; the school can demonstrate respect for the ways that parents do things with their child and acknowledge the skills that children bring to the setting.

Jindal-Snape (2010) suggests that it is up to the professionals to learn to implement strategies according to individuals' needs and their ways of dealing with transition. The right amount of information (both given and received), timing of discussions and the level of accessibility (both pre- and post-transfer) can instil parents with confidence in the school, reduce stress and make learning accessible (Fabian 2002). Parents usually want to know about pragmatic aspects, such as what is expected of them on the first day of school, where their child hangs their coat, what happens if their child is ill, where they wait at the end of the day and so on. Therefore, during visits to school it is helpful if parents are given information (both verbal and written) about how to access the teacher and guidance about school rules and routines, and also that they discuss expectations about their role.

To increase their agency, children need to be asked about what they want, have time to talk about their expectations and for staff to inform them about school. One example of this is through the use of a child-sized school-uniformed puppet that answers the children's questions, shows them photographs of the classroom, teaches songs about starting school and puts forward problems to discuss that 'he' has encountered at school (Office for Standards in Education 2012).

This section has emphasised that good communication between all parties eases the induction to school. Information flow helps children and parents to understand the next stage of education and helps teachers to understand the child's level of attainment at the start of school.

Summary

This chapter has outlined transition theory that informs practice through the themes of learning, sociocultural understanding, emotional well-being and communication. The theory draws mainly on the work of van Gennep, Bronfenbrenner and Bruner, to demonstrate that entry to school is an important life event but that transitions are an individual process and need to be personalised if each child is going to settle into school easily and gain resilience for future transitions.

Starting school can be seen as an exciting time that involves a number of people working together, a time of growing up and one that children and their parents generally view positively, as there are usually high hopes at the start of school. It is much easier to settle and be confident if all those involved have communicated together beforehand, discussed expectations and scaffolded the process by providing relevant experiences, establishing positive relationships and making the culture meaningful.

Children have a vague idea of what to expect from school but are usually convinced they are going to do well. However, if they are going to settle quickly into their new setting and continue learning without too many hiccups then they need to be helped to visualise the new situation and plan for change. Border zones, between knowing and becoming, harmonise change and empower children to navigate their way through the structures to enable risk-taking and to learn from mistakes, to build a positive self-image and to develop the capacity to interact with others. There are links between socio-emotional well-being and cognitive development, so fostering friendships is likely to bring about positive notions of school and the confidence to learn. By staying in touch with established relationships, children can 'keep anchored' and be encouraged to respect cultures on either side of the border.

Parents also have a change of role when their child starts school but by co-constructing the transition, family circumstances can be taken into account and all participants can feel valued and respected as individuals in the 'schoolification' process.

Schools should have policies in place to support smooth transitions and curriculum continuity and a regular review process to keep them up to date and owned by those involved. The transition process cannot be hurried. Children will go through an incubation period – gradually taking on the cultural identity of the school by watching and taking part – and arrive at feeling 'suitable' (Broström 2002: 52), unaware and without conscious effort.

References

Anning, A. and Edwards, A. (2006) *Promoting Children's Learning from Birth to Five: Developing the New Early Years Professional* (2nd edn.), Maidenhead: Open University Press.

Ball, C. (1994) *Start Right: The Importance of Early Learning*, London: The Royal Society for the Encouragement of Arts, Manufactures and Commerce.

Bowlby, J. (1988) *A Secure Base: Parent–Child Attachment and Healthy Human Development*, London: Routledge.

Bronfenbrenner, U. (1979) *The Ecology of Human Development: Experiments by Nature and Design*, Cambridge: Harvard University Press.

Brooker, L. (2002) *Starting School: Young Children Learning Cultures*, Buckingham, UK: Open University Press.

Brooker, L. (2008) *Supporting Transitions in the Early Years*, London: McGraw-Hill.

Broström, S. (2002) 'Communication and continuity in the transition from kindergarten to school', in H. Fabian and A.W. Dunlop (eds.) *Transitions in the Early Years: Debating Continuity and Progression for Children in Early Education*, London: RoutledgeFalmer.

Bruner, J.S. (1996) *The Culture of Education*, Cambridge: Harvard University Press.

Campbell Clark, S. (2000) 'Work/family border theory: A new theory of work/family balance', *Human Relations* 53(6): 747–770.

Cefai, C. (2008) *Promoting Resilience in the Classroom: A Guide to Developing Pupils' Emotional and Cognitive Skills*, London: Jessica Kingsley.

Cowan, P.A. and Hetherington, E.M. (eds.) (1991) *Family Transitions: Advances in Family Research*, Hillsdale, NJ: Lawrence Erlbaum Associates.

Csikszentmihalyi, M. (1990) *Flow: The Psychology of Optimal Experience*, New York: Harper & Row.

Dencik, L. (2006) 'Parent–child relationships in early childhood in contemporary welfare societies'. Paper presented at European Early Childhood Research Association Conference, Reykjavik, Iceland, 30 August–2 September 2006.

Department for Education (2012) *Statutory Framework for the Early Years Foundation Stage 2012*, Norwich: The Stationery Office.

Department for Education and Science (2003) 'The Framework for Children's Services in England', *Every Child Matters*, Norwich: The Stationery Office.

Dockett, S. and Perry, B. (2007) 'Children's transition to school: Changing expectations', in A.W. Dunlop and H. Fabian (eds.) *Informing Transitions: Research, Policy and Practice*, Berkshire: Open University Press/McGraw-Hill.

Dunlop, A.W. (2007) 'Bridging research, policy and practice', in A.W. Dunlop and H. Fabian (eds.) *Informing Transitions: Research, Policy and Practice*, Berkshire: Open University Press/McGraw-Hill.

Edwards, A. and Knight, P. (1994) *Effective Early Years Education*, Buckingham: Open University Press.

Einarsdottir, J. (2003) 'When the bell rings we have to go inside: Pre-school children's views on the primary school', *European Early Childhood Education Research Journal: Themed Monograph: Transitions Series* 1: 35–49.

Fabian, H. (2002) *Children Starting School: A Guide to Successful Transitions and Transfers for Teachers and Assistants*, London: David Fulton.

Fabian, H. (2007) 'The challenges of starting school', in J.R. Moyles (ed.) *Early Years Foundations: Meeting the Challenge*, Maidenhead: Open University Press/McGraw-Hill.

Fabian, H. and Dunlop, A.W. (2005) 'The importance of play in transitions', in J.R. Moyles (ed.) *The Excellence of Play* (2nd edn.), Berkshire: Open University Press/McGraw-Hill.

Fabian, H. and Dunlop, A.W. (2010) 'Personalising transitions: How play can help "newly arrived children" settle into school', in J.R. Moyles (ed.) *The Excellence of Play* (3rd edn.), Maidenhead: Open University Press/McGraw-Hill.

Goleman, D. (1996) *Emotional Intelligence*, London: Bloomsbury Publishing.

Griebel, W. and Niesel, R. (2002) 'Co-constructing transition into kindergarten and school by children, parents, and teachers', in H. Fabian and A.W. Dunlop (eds.) *Transition in the Early Years*, London: RoutledgeFalmer.

Hamre, B.K. and Pianta, R.C. (2001) 'Early teacher–child relationships and the trajectory of children's school outcomes through eighth grade', *Child Development* 72(2): 625–638.

Jindal-Snape, D. (ed.) (2010) *Educational Transitions: Moving Stories from around the World*, Oxford: Routledge.

Johansson, I. (2002) 'Parents' views of transition to school and their influence in this process', in H. Fabian and A.W. Dunlop (eds.) *Transitions in the Early Years: Debating Continuity and Progression for Children in Early Education*, London: RoutledgeFalmer.

Krovetz, M.L. (1999) *Fostering Resiliency*, Thousand Oaks, CA: Corwin Press.

Ladd, G.W. (2003) 'School transitions/school readiness: An outcome of early childhood development', in R.E. Tremblay, R.G. Barr and R. DeV. Peters (eds.) *Encyclopaedia on Early Childhood Development* (pp. 1–10), Montreal, Quebec: Centre of Excellence for Early Childhood Development. Online, available at: <http://www.child-encyclopedia.com/documents/LaddANGxp.pdf> (accessed 12 April 2012).

Laevers, F., Vandenbussche, E., Kog, M. and Depondt, L. (1997) *A Process-Oriented Child Monitoring System for Young Children*, Leuven: Centre for Experiential Education, Katholieke Universiteit.

Margetts, K. (2002) 'Transition to school – complexity and diversity', *European Early Childhood Education Research Journal* 10(2): 103–114.

Mayall, B. (2007) *Children's Lives Outside School and Their Educational Impact* (Primary Review Research Survey 8/1), Cambridge: University of Cambridge Faculty of Education.

Newman, T. and Blackburn, S. (2002) *Interchange 78 Transitions in the Lives of Children and Young People: Resilience Factors*, Edinburgh: Scottish Executive Education Department.

Niesel, R. and Griebel, W. (2005) 'Transition competence and resiliency in educational institutions', *International Journal of Transitions in Childhood* 1: 25–33.

Niesel, R. and Griebel, W. (2007) 'Enhancing the competence of transition systems through co-construction', in A.W. Dunlop and H. Fabian (eds.) *Informing Transitions in the Early Years: Research, Policy and Practice*, Berkshire: Open University Press, McGraw-Hill Education.

Nutbrown, C. (ed.) (1996) *Respectful Educators – Capable Learners: Children's Rights and Early Education*, London: Paul Chapman Publishing.

Office for Standards in Education (2012) *Early Years Foundation Stage to School Transition Project: Carousel Children's Centre* (URN 20386, Ref. 120043). Online, available at: http://www.ofsted.gov.uk/sites/default/files/documents/surveys-and-good-practice/c/Carousel%20Children%27s%20Centre%20-%20Good%20practice%20example.pdf (accessed June 2012).

Peters, S. (2010) 'Shifting the lens: Re-framing the view of learners and learning during the transition from early childhood education to school in New Zealand', in D. Jindal-Snape (ed.) *Educational Transitions: Moving Stories from around the World* (pp. 8–84), Oxford: Routledge.

Rutter, M. and Rutter, M. (1992) *Developing Minds: Challenge and Continuity Across the Life Span*, London: Penguin.

Van Gennep, A. (1960) *Rites of Passage*, trans. by M.B. Vizedom and G.L. Caffee, London: Routledge & Kegan Paul.

6

TRANSITION TO SCHOOL

Contemporary Danish perspectives

Anders Skriver Jensen, Ole Henrik Hansen and Stig Broström

This chapter involves two parts: an introduction to the Danish day care and school system plus theory and practice on children's language acquisition. In the first part we describe the legislative basis for transition to school and typical transition activities used in Danish municipalities. In addition we refer to an investigation on children's expectations about school. In the second part, because a claim for the development of children's language competences (school readiness) is seen as an underlying dimension, we focus on children's language acquisition. Based on Michael Tomasello's (2003, 2008) theory of language, emphasising joint attention and intersubjectivity, we describe the dimensions of educational practice that might contribute to the development of children's language.

Legislation to ease and optimise the transition from day care to school

Denmark currently has one of the world's highest percentages of day care enrollment. Day care for infants up to 3 years of age and day care for preschoolers from 3 to 6 years of age are often viewed as a whole and termed day care services. About 95 per cent of 3- to 5-year-olds are enrolled in day care, and the majority of children (98 per cent between 6 and 8 years attend leisure-time centres (Danmarks Statistik 2009)). Leisure-time centres are an integrated part of the public schools and are for children outside school hours and in vacation times. The centres are closely aligned to schools; the pedagogues are involved with the children's transition to school and work closely with the teachers at school. However, the leisure-time centre is an independent institution with its own curricula emphasising play and children's self-governed activity. The legislative framework is the *Act on Day Care Services* (Retsinformation 2007).

The year a child turns 6 years old their compulsory education begins. They have the right to be enrolled free of charge in kindergarten in public school – according to the *Act on the Folkeskole*, which covers primary and lower secondary education (Retsinformation 2009). The first year in school is called Grade 0 or kindergarten and the legislative intentions are that lessons should mainly be structured in play-like ways.

Although two different Acts govern day care services and public schools, there is ongoing work to inscribe, in both laws, matters that ease and optimise the transition from day care to school. At present, the two Acts contain many similarities and phrases that are intended to promote this transition – and the related pedagogical practices – as joint efforts, involving collaboration between early childhood educators and caregivers (referred to as 'pedagogues' in the Danish context) in day care centres and teachers in Grades 0 (kindergarten) to 2 in public school. (The training for day care pedagogues is three and a half years and they graduate with a professional bachelor degree. Their training emphasises children's development, care and education. The training for teachers in primary school is four years, and emphasises education, curriculum theory and specific subject areas as major subjects. Teachers also graduate with a professional bachelor degree. Teachers in kindergarten are pedagogues who have received further training.) The democratic dimension is clearly stated in both Acts and both settings, as is the requirement to provide children with academic skills, general competences and opportunities for diverse, personal development.

As a final note on the legislative phrases, day care services – in collaboration with parents – are responsible for facilitating a 'good transition to school' (Retsinformation 2007). The nurturing of 1) basic competences and 2) general motivation towards learning is thought to do this.

On the central level some requirements for children's transition are described. The Ministry of Education and Ministry of Welfare (2008) produced a guidebook on the transition in order to optimise children's school commencement, aimed at the municipalities, the parents, the school teachers and day care service pedagogues. (From 2012 the two ministries are united in The Ministry of Children and Education.) Although day care and school have two different curricula – the *Act on Educational Curricula* from 2004 and the *Shared Aims in Kindergarten* from 2009 respectively – the two ministries have composed these curricula with progression in aims and content related to the same general themes, where first of all children's language acquisition is prioritised.

On the local level, during the last ten years, more and more municipalities have developed a policy on transition to school and established transition strategies in order to achieve continuity and progression between day care centres and school. Typically four forms of continuity are seen (Broström 2002):

1. Curricula development or pedagogical and programme continuity: to design a coordinated curriculum for the day care service, kindergarten and the leisure- time centre.
2. Administrative continuity: the establishment of a joint administrative organisation, which includes both strategies and initiatives taken by the municipal administration and initiatives taken by the head of the school and the leadership of the day care centre and leisure-time centre.
3. Personal or professional interaction: here pedagogues and teachers cooperate and carry out mutual activities (see below).
4. Continuity with parents: establishment of coherence with homes through activities that invite parents to be involved in school life and learn about the school and their child's well-being and learning.

A survey of a number of randomly selected municipalities in May 2010 showed that about 70 per cent have a transition policy containing shared overall aims, written objectives and guidelines for the cooperation between day care and school. The municipalities also require day care centres and schools to establish a number of transition activities, which the Danish Government's so-called *School Start Commission* described in a report in 2007 (Broström 2007). These include the following:

- During the last year before starting school, the future school children are gathered in a so-called 'school group' and given relevant challenges.
- The school invites the child and their parents to visit the leisure-time centre and kindergarten before the start of school.
- The day care service pedagogues and children visit kindergarten before the start of school in order to get a better understanding of school.
- The day care service pedagogues and children visit the leisure-time centre.
- The prospective kindergarten teacher visits the children in their day care centre.
- The day care service pedagogues and kindergarten teachers collaborate on a local document defining school readiness.
- The day care service pedagogues and kindergarten teachers have dialogues with parents about the individual child's school readiness.
- The day care service pedagogues and kindergarten teachers have meetings before the start of school about children's lives, development and school readiness.
- Children and day care service pedagogues are involved in a number of lessons in kindergarten before the start of school.

The implementation of such transition activities can help children to develop a realistic understanding of what school is and what happens in school, which may ease their transition to school.

Children's expectations about school

In spite of children in many municipalities being involved in a number of the above-mentioned transition activities, some children in day care services have little insight into what will happen in kindergarten, as is expressed in a Danish study of children's expectations about school (Broström 2001). Researchers interviewed 375 children before they started school concerning their expectations about school. Children were asked, 'What do you think you will do at school' and 'What do you think you will learn at school?'. In brief, the study showed that 50 per cent of the children expressed a school-oriented expectation, 6 per cent expressed a day-care-oriented expectation, 33 per cent expressed a combination and 11 per cent expressed no expectations. School expectations were characterised by a wish to learn to read and write, while day care expectations focused on play and self-governed and aesthetic activities. Combination expectations reflected both dimensions. The examples below illustrate the kinds of responses given by the children in each category.

> A boy of 6.4 years expressed a *school-oriented* expectation: 'Maths, reading, maths, counting. We will learn how to write. You have to figure out what the writing means, because then you can understand the numbers, and then you get smart.'

> A girl of 5.5 years had a *day care* expectation: 'We will draw and play, pick flowers and sit nicely around the table and eat our lunch. Also climb trees. Maybe read a little. I don't know. We will learn to play and not to fight. And if some boys come we can play "girls against boys". And maybe we will make birds with glue, and I don't know what else.'

> A boy of 5.7 years from a different ethnic background than Danish expressed a *combination expectation*: 'Draw, cut, play football, play with other children, play with beads, play outside, also bike. Learn to speak Danish, learn to play with Danish children, learn to write my name.'

No doubt most children have an expectation about learning to read and write at school. This reflects the idea of school readiness being associated with early literacy, and represents what happens in school.

Awareness of language acquisition as a usage-based process

Children's expectations are as indicated above: a complex of social and cultural factors, some of which can relate to the child's earliest experiences in day care. Therefore, it is crucial that the day care centre is able to facilitate the necessary personal care and well-being as well as an age-relevant educational content.

One of the things that is believed to pave the way for transitional competences that lead to school readiness is an early effort to develop the child's linguistic skills (Hansen 2010b).

Preliminary data from research on the youngest children (Hansen 2010a) imply that the implementation of such national tests, as well as a strong political effort to promote Denmark as a country with high quality lifelong education for all children, brings about an unintended pedagogical practice in the day care centres. In some cases, pedagogues assign a lower priority to crucial care elements such as the child's perspective, empathy and the importance of intersubjectivity and lived situations, but also the mastering of objects and social phenomena. Instead, the educational focus turns into an unintended asymmetric approach in which the transfer of primarily linguistic curricula and testable competences are in focus and the child is limited in his or her abilities in attachment and intersubjectivity. Such a focus is a paradox, given the Danish pedagogues' traditional reluctance towards teaching. The approach fits in poorly with the Nordic socio-pedagogic tradition and is unlikely to be the intention of the ministries and administrators responsible.

Rather than making too sharp a contrast, it seems advisable to combine the two approaches, one merging into the other, as part of the same continuum. At one end are broad developmental goals such as motor- and socio-emotional development, and authentic lived contextual approaches to culture and social skills – the so-called Nordic socio-educational model. At the other end is the emphasis on structured and academic activities, where lived experience tends to play a secondary role (OECD 2006).

Research implies that a one-sided curriculum approach in which democratic and social life plays a secondary role can be problematic because young children's language acquisition is primarily facilitated by the possibility of role reversal imitation, due to elements such as closeness, empathy, imitation and multimodality in a zone of joint attention (Tomasello 2008). First and foremost, children from language-poor home environments may not achieve age-appropriate linguistic skills. Research emphasises that language is acquired by use and reflects two views: a) 'meaning is use', which aims to focus on how children use linguistic conventions to achieve social goals, and b) 'structure emerges from use', as an attempt to focus on how meaning-based grammatical constructions emerge from individual acts of language use (Tomasello 2008, 2009). Utilising these two key views as an underlying basis, children come to the process of language acquisition with abilities in intentional reading and pattern finding (Tomasello 2009). Intentional reading is what the child must do to comprehend the processes and goals of mature users of linguistic conventions. Pattern finding is what the child must do to go beyond the individual utterances they hear people use. Pattern finding is overall the most central cognitive construct in the usage-based approach to language acquisition (Tomasello 2003, 2008, 2009).

Almost all infants communicate non-verbally, for example, by pointing, before they acquire any productive oral language (Tomasello 2009). An interesting thing about pointing is that the gesture itself has no information attached to it. The meaning comes through use in mutually understood contextual settings. For example, if a pre-linguistic child is engaged in an activity with an adult and the adult points to an object across the room, the child will assume it is related to their shared attention and fetch the object, but if another person enters the room and points at the object, the child will not respond (Tomasello 2009). Thus even pre-linguistic infants do not just communicate about what they understand about the world, but mostly about their shared understandings with communicative partners. Even at a very young age, children have the ability to construct such shared understandings. This is also the way children learn words: they do not primarily try to learn them directly but try to determine the functional role they play (Tomasello 2009). This implies that a child's communicative abilities are explored in intersubjective frames of joint attention, and their language abilities are very individual, depending on very complex contextual, social and cultural conditions that determine the child's language.

Children in transition

Taking the perspective of a child engaged in transition, the focus must relate to different sorts of linguistic process (vocabulary, communication, etc.) and at the same time identify which influential elements drive these processes (Hansen 2010a). So what is essential for the youngest children is not testing their competences or focusing on a one-sided curriculum approach, but rather emphasising elements such as imitation, empathy, multimodal interactions and the ability to create meaningful frames of joint attention, where children and adults are given the time and space to develop close, empathic relations.

As children grow up, they are expected to learn to read and write. When they make the transition from day care to school, some of them can hardly spell their name, while others have come far in experimenting with signs and symbols. How can pedagogues and teachers approach early literacy in ways that continue the focus on empathy, as we have just outlined, while discussing the usage-based approach to language acquisition? Is it possible to merge social competences and democratic dimensions with the teaching of reading and writing skills? And what do the teachers and pedagogues think about their own pedagogic practices in relation to early literacy as a transition phenomenon?

Early literacy and transition to school: Beyond the acquisition of skills

We will draw on some fresh data to shed light on the questions above. Meet Rebecca, who is currently teaching Danish in second grade. The following text is an excerpt from an interview with her, which was conducted as part of a current research project on early literacy in relation to the transition to school. The overarching goal of the project is to establish a unified approach to early literacy that stretches from day care services up to second grade in school (children approximately 0–9 years of age). Consider the passage below in which Rebecca relates what she thinks is important in her teaching practice.

> The room you are in together. The **common room** and the **social room** you are in together are tremendously significant with regards to daring to learn together. And when I say dare it is because I really believe that we can create such a [**room**] … I can see it in my class at this time. The children are at **very different places** with regards to their academic performance and their personal development, so to be able to be together in a relevant kind of way, we need a **room** without prejudice. Those who are 'super duper bright', who are racing down that path, reading Harry Potter now, they need to learn it as well. They need to think that those who are landing from the moon sometimes are asking important questions as well. They should not just conceive of it as a necessary evil, but more generally speaking, the more **it** [**the social room**] is opened up, also opened for wonder, the better a place it is to learn together.

Let us have a closer look at what she is saying here. We have enboldened the term 'social room' to draw attention to the room and spatial metaphors that run through the passage. Three times Rebecca explicitly invokes the concept of room in different ways, and at three other times it is being assumed but not articulated, including a reference to being in different places (in relation to each other – spatiality/room). All occurrences are enboldened for clarification. Having established 'a social room' as a central concept for her teaching practice, it is possible for Rebecca to work with early literacy as something tied to the social practices in the classroom, thus moving beyond the level of individual skill acquisition. This is a sociocultural (or social–semiotic) approach to early literacy (Gee 2001; Kress 1997; Lave & Wenger 1991; Street 1995).

Having acknowledged the social and communicative nature of early literacy, it seems obvious to take a stance on the issue of equal *opportunities to learn* (Gee 2003). This is articulated by Rebecca when she stresses the need to get rid of prejudice in order for the children to be able to dare together, and thus to learn together. Rebecca, as the teacher, needs to be a role model, relying on the children's perspectives instead of her power (as an adult and a teacher) to define right from wrong (Bae 1996; Rinaldi 2006). 'Daring and learning together' situates issues related to opportunities to learn in the midst of the early literacy teaching and learning processes. In practice, this is of course no easy task, and it puts a tremendous amount of responsibility on the children. The children need to develop social competencies regarding tolerance and mutual recognition along with communicative competences, including the ability to think critically in democratic and solidary ways (Broström 2006b; Giroux 2001; Klafki 2001).

Further developing this angle, we can assume that Rebecca values diversity in her early literacy teaching, but she is aware that respect and mutual recognition are things that need to be taught alongside formal skills (Broström 2006a). This is indicated when she stresses that those who are 'super duper bright' *need to* recognise the contributions of classmates who are not yet racing down that (reading) path. This is similar to Honneth's (2003, 2006) discussion of a broad horizon of recognition.

Children's experiences outside school (in home-, peer- and pop-culture-based domains) are seen as holding considerable promise regarding early literacy (Fast 2009; Gee 2004, 2008; Perregaard 2003). While Rebecca does not explicitly say (in the previous passage, at least) that she is working on bringing the different domains of the children into her teaching, she stresses that she wants the children to develop an awareness of each other's perspectives:

> [The classmates] need to think that those who are landing from the moon [those who are sometimes out of sync with the current literacy event] sometimes ask important questions as well. They should not just conceive of it [the question posed by an 'out of sync' classmate] as a necessary evil.

We have used Rebecca's own words together with an analysis to point to ways of conceiving of early literacy teaching that are not only well backed by research but also hold considerable promise regarding connections between social and communicative competences. When learning to be together is seen as part and parcel of learning to read and write, it might contribute to a successful transition to school, as the social pedagogy approach of the day care service is merged into the academic world of school (Jensen 2010). This claim is speculation at this time, but it is a question central to the research project on early literacy and transition to school, from which the passage with Rebecca is taken. In any case, the analysis has exemplified what a unity of care, upbringing and teaching might look like from the school side of the transition and thus adds to the ongoing work to revitalise the social pedagogy approach to meet the demands of a changing world (Broström 2006a, 2006b, 2009).

Educational practice in day care service and school

Language education in day care services must be based on the traditions of the day care services but at the same time, in order to smooth transition, must reach out to education in school, namely to a focus on oral language (listening and speaking), written language (reading and writing) plus literature and communication. *Oral language* is stimulated when the day care service pedagogues respond to children's curiosity and questions and invite children to participate in dialogues and communication. Stimulation occurs in many formal and informal situations during the day; however, pedagogues must use educational creativity in order to reach all children. For example, some shy and reserved children may have a language breakthrough if, for example, a pedagogue and some children transform a cardboard box into a TV. This may give quiet children the courage to read the news and tell stories because they feel secure behind the box.

In day care services, children are also involved with *written language*. Their first written language is expressed via their drawings, where they symbolise objects, persons and phenomena from the surrounding world (Vygotsky 1978). Then they realise that they are able to draw speech, in other words, to create characters for speech. Typically, children scribble, they pretend they are writing the whole story and step by step they insert 'real' characters as a first step in the development of conventional writing. This happens for example when the pedagogues read challenging stories and ask them to write a story themselves and also when she/he invites children to do drawings expressed as comic strip with text below.

Five-year-olds may do word cards and play with their favourite words. Together with the pedagogue they may also write shopping lists related to a play theme or cooking experience. The pedagogue may also introduce written language into their play, for example, by providing prescriptions in a doctor game and a pad to write fines on in a police game (Christie 1991). At that stage, they must be encouraged to combine drawing and written language at a higher level, namely to produce cartoons based on a template with three squares for text and drawings – beginning, middle and end.

Another approach to early literacy in day care service with reference to teaching in school is the use of *children's literature*. A number of researchers find reading to preschoolers to be an important influence on children's language development and also later general reading abilities (Scarborough & Dobrich 1994; Sénéchal & LeFevre 2002; Silvén, Ahtola & Niemi 2003). Findings also indicate that reading together in day care has a positive effect on children's storytelling if it includes dialogues about the books and working with the literature via role-play and drawing (Anning 2003; Pellegrini & Galda 1998, Silvén et al. 2003).

Based on the hypothesis that reading of fiction combined with aesthetic reflections and expression in the form of children's storytelling, drawing and play might be a useful tool in developing children's literacy, Broström together with four day care centres and one school, in spring before school start, carried out a developmental research project that at the same time aimed to support the children's transition to school. The project was based on the following approach (Broström 2010):

1. A day care service pedagogue (or the children's future teacher) reads aloud a short story of high literary quality.
2. Based on the story, the pedagogue involves children in a structured conversation (Chambers 1994) called a *literature dialogue*.
3. After the dialogue the children *make drawings* to illustrate their understanding of the text, and they also fill in their own writings.
4. Arranged in formal groups, the children are challenged to turn their literature experiences into *playing*. The pedagogue has the role of observer and also participates as 'pedagogue-in-role'.
5. Sometimes the pedagogue asks the children to present their version of the story for their classmates and other pedagogues.
6. After the presentation, the pedagogues and each play group hold a structured conversation called a *learning dialogue*.
7. During all phases, the pedagogues and the children engage in *philosophical dialogues* reflecting their ideas.

Selection of books of high quality must be related to the context, to the specific children's lives, but also combined with some general criteria: the children must be able to identify themselves with the main character. The story must have some subordinate characters and some appealing anti-heroes in order to make a shift in perspectives to promote reflection. It must open for empathic involvement and also challenge children with new and unfamiliar experiences, and finally help children to create meaning and coherence in their life.

In the developmental work among other books, children were introduced to five books in the series *Miss Ignora*. Ignora is a girl living alone in a water tower without her father and mother. Sometimes she loses her temper and explodes in front of her teacher; then her best friend Nina becomes afraid and Ignora is sorry. Sometimes she speaks with her neighbour, a fishmonger from whom she also occasionally steals fish, which she feeds to the cats. In the schoolyard she is scolded and bullied by a boy, George, who later becomes her best friend, etc., etc. The stories are told in simple, rhythmical and unsentimental language, and they display strong emotions that all children experience: friendship, anger, happiness, sorrow, shyness, disappointment and love.

After a reading session in the children's school-to-be, the pedagogues and the new school teacher introduced the first *Miss Ignora* book and they arranged a structured conversation – a so-called *literature dialogue* – about the stories inspired by Chambers (1994), who proposes that children be asked a number of questions to which each child should respond: 1) Did you find elements in the story that you liked? 2) Did you find something that you disliked? 3) Did you find something that surprised you? 4) Did you find patterns in the story that you recognised, which reminded you of other stories? The children's answers and later the drawing and play sessions are reported elsewhere (Broström 2010). However, the aim of the literature conversation is to support children's own reflection processes and to prepare them for the subsequent drawing and play sessions. The literature conversation focuses on academic literature knowledge, but the day care service pedagogue or teacher has to create a balance with children's own experiences and understanding and give space for children's mutual exchange, which often crosses the universe of the story.

The emphasis on children's reflection via literature dialogue, drawings and play is aimed at developing a new psychological structure in the child's mind, namely the development of the child's learning motive and meta-cognition (Leont'ev 1981). The establishment of a learning motive implies a motivation that goes beyond the current situation. Thus we assume that an active use of literature conversation, drawing and play will have an impact on the development of higher mental functions. Among other things, children's learning motive seems to be strengthening their possibility to gain from the more structured learning environment in school. Thus, the involved early literacy activities can also be seen as transitory activities.

Final remarks: Towards a new paradigm in early childhood education and care

We have discussed some contemporary issues in relation to the transition to school in Denmark. It is clear that approaches in day care services and schools are inscribed in a policy that intends to ease the transition. Despite this continuity-oriented policy, some children feel anxious when they are about to make the transition. This anxiety stems from images of scolding teachers and rigid authoritarian learning environments that are out of sync with reality in Danish schools. Continuing the interest in children's perspectives, we have sketched some key elements in sociocultural approaches to language acquisition and early literacy, where communicative competences are seen as interwoven with dimensions of empathy, the social setting and an overall pedagogical sensitivity towards the child as a maker of meaning. We have sketched some hands-on, child-focused approaches to teaching language and literacy in day care and the first years of school.

The arguments in this chapter rest on a firm belief in the importance of rethinking the traditional approaches to early childhood education. In Denmark, transition bridges day care services, leisure-time centres and schools at a time when standardisation of curricula and testing is on the rise. What is sorely needed is a theoretical and practical approach that unifies the concepts of care, upbringing and education in an attempt to further develop the strengths of the social pedagogy approach while answering the challenge of globalisation (Broström 2006a, 2006b, 2009; Hansen 2010b; Jensen 2010; OECD 2001, 2006).

References

Anning, A. (2003) 'Pathways to the graphicacy club: The crossroad of home and preschool', *Journal of Early Childhood Literacy* 3: 5–35.

Bae, B. (1996) 'Voksnes definitionsmagt og børns selvoplevelse' [The adults' power to define and children's conceptions of themselves], *Social Kritik* 47: 6–21.

Broström, S. (2001) *Børns Forventninger til Skolen – en Forskningsrapport* [Children's expectations to school, a research report], Copenhagen: DPU.

Broström, S. (2002) 'Communication and continuity in the transition from kindergarten to school', in H. Fabian, and A.W. Dunlop (ed.) *Transitions in the Early Years: Debating Continuity and Progression for Children in Early Education*, London: RoutledgeFalmer Education.

Broström, S. (2006a) 'Care and education: Towards a new paradigm in early childhood education', *Child and Youth Care Forum* 35: 391–409.

Broström, S. (2006b) 'Education to democracy: A possible approach to early childhood education?' Paper presented at 34th Nordic Educational Research Association Annual Conference, Örebro, March 2006.

Broström, S. (2007) 'Overgang fra dagtilbud til skole', in N. Egelund (ed.) *Skolestart. Udfordringer for Daginstitution, Sskole og Fritidsordning*, Vejle: Krogs Forlag.

Broström, S. (2009) 'Tilpasning, frigjøring og demokrati', *Første Steg* 2: 24–28.

Broström, S. (2010) 'Fiction, drawing and play in a Vygotskian perspective', in J. Hayden and A. Tuna (eds.) *Moving Forward Together: Early Childhood Programs as the Doorway to Social Cohesion. An East-West Perspective*, Cambridge: Cambridge Scholars Publishing.

Chambers, A. (1994) *Tell Me: Children Reading and Talk*, Stroud: The Thimble Press.

Christie, J.F. (1991) *Play and Early Literacy Development*, New York: State University of New York Press.

Danmarks Statistik (2009) *Danmarks Statistik*. Online, available at: <http://www.danmarksstatistik.dk/www.danmarksstatistik.dk> (accessed May 2012).

Fast, C. (2009) *Literacy – i Familie, Børnehave og Skole* [Literacy – in Family, Daycare and School], København: Gyldendal.

Gee, J.P. (2001) 'A sociocultural perspective on early literacy development', in S.B. Neumann and D.K. Dickinson (eds.) *Handbook of Early Literacy Research* (Vol. 1), New York: Guilford Press.

Gee, J.P. (2003) 'Opportunity to learn: A language-based perspective on assessment', *Assessment in Education* 10(1): 27–46.

Gee, J.P. (2004) *Situated Language and Learning: A Critique of Traditional Schooling*, New York: Routledge.

Gee, J.P. (2008) *Social Linguistics and Literacies: Ideology in Discourses* (3rd edn.), London: Taylor & Francis.

Giroux, H.A. (2001) *Theory and Resistance in Education*, Westport, CT: Bergin & Garvey.

Hansen, O.H. (2010a) 'Det postmoderne barn' [The postmodern child], *Dansk Paedagogist Forum* 0–14(2): 50–56.

Hansen, O.H. (2010b) 'Early language and thought'. Paper presented at the 26th OMEP World Congress, Göteborg, Sweden, 11–13 August 2010.

Honneth, A. (2003) *Behovet for Anerkendelse* [The need for recognition], København: Hans Reitzels Forlag.

Honneth, A. (2006) *Kamp om Anerkendelse* [Fight for recognition], København: Hans Reitzels Forlag.

Jensen, A.S. (2010) 'Early literacy and inclusion'. Paper presented at the 26th OMEP World Congress, Göteborg, Sweden, 11–13 August 2010.

Klafki, W. (2001) *Dannelsesteori og Didaktik – Nye Studier* [Educational Theory and Didaktik – New Studies], Århus: Klim.

Kress, G. (1997) *Before Writing: Rethinking the Paths to Literacy*, London: Routledge.

Lave, J. and Wenger, E. (1991) *Situated Learning*, Cambridge: Cambridge University Press.

Leont'ev, A.N. (1981) *Problems of the Development of the Mind*, Moscow: Progress Publishers.

Ministry of Education and Ministry of Welfare (2008). *På vej til Skole* [Transition to School], Denmark: Velfærdsministeriet og Undervisningsministeriet.

OECD (2001) *Starting Strong: Early Education and Care*, Paris: OECD.

OECD (2006) *Starting Strong 2*, Paris: OECD.

Pellegrini, A.D. and Galda, L. (1998) *The Development of School-Based Literacy: A Social Ecological Perspective*, London: Routledge.

Perregaard, B. (2003) *Må Vi Skrive på Vores Historie?* [May We Write on Our Story?], København: Akademisk Forlag.

Retsinformation (2007) *Dagtilbudsloven* [Act on Day Care Services]. Online, available at: <https://www.retsinformation.dk/> (accessed June 2012).

Retsinformation (2009) *Folkeskoleloven* (LBK 593, 24/06/2009) [Act on Public School]. Online, available at: <https://www.retsinformation.dk/> (accessed June 2012).

Rinaldi, C. (2006) *In Dialogue with Reggio Emilia: Listening, Researching and Learning*, London: Routledge.

Scarborough, S.H. and Dobrich, W. (1994) 'On the efficacy of reading to preschoolers', *Developmental Review* 14: 245–302.

Sénéchal, M. and LeFevre, J. (2002) 'Parental involvement in the development of children's reading skill: A five-year longitudinal study', *Child Development* 73(2): 445–460.

Silvén, M., Ahtola, A. and Niemi, P. (2003) 'Early words, multiword utterances and maternal reading strategies as predictors of mastering word inflections in Finnish', *Journal of Child Language* 30: 253–279.

Street, B.V. (1995) *Social Literacies: Critical Approaches to Literacy in Development, Ethnography and Education*, Real Language Series, New York: Longman.

Tomasello, M. (2003) *Constructing a Language*, Cambridge: Harvard University Press.

Tomasello, M. (2008) 'Origins of human communication', *The Jean Nicod Lectures 2008* xiii: 393.

Tomasello, M. (2009) 'The usage-based theory of language acquisition', in E.L. Bavin (ed.) *The Cambridge Handbook of Child Language*, Cambridge: Cambridge University Press.

Vygotsky, L.S. (1978) 'The prehistory of written language', in M. Cole, V. John-Steiner, S. Scribner and E. Souberman (eds.) *Mind in Society. The Development of Higher Psychological Processes*. Cambridge: Harvard University Press.

7

TRANSITION FROM PRESCHOOL TO PRIMARY SCHOOL IN ICELAND FROM THE PERSPECTIVES OF CHILDREN

Johanna Einarsdottir

Children are the key players in transition to school. This chapter discusses children's perspectives, expectations and experiences of starting primary school. In the Nordic countries, almost all children have attended preschool for several years before they start primary school, and in Iceland, preschool is the first level of schooling. Although preschool attendance is nearly universal today, there is a considerable difference between preschool and primary school levels. They have very different histories, traditions and organisation, and the laws and national curricula governing them have different emphases. This chapter builds on four studies conducted with children in preschools and primary schools in Iceland. Analysis of the findings conveyed several themes: the children saw changes in their status and responsibilities, in the teaching methods and in the level of democracy; they had been prepared for these changes in preschool and by society; they defined learning that took place in primary school but not in preschool; and they missed other children and time to play in preschool.

Introduction

Preschools and primary schools in Iceland have different histories and build on different traditions. The first day care centres in Iceland were established during the beginning of urbanisation in the 1920s. Designed as a response to the need to feed and shelter poor children and to keep them off the streets, the first day care centres aimed to provide the children with warmth, wholesome nourishment, and hygiene. The main aims of the primary school, on the other hand, were to teach children to read and write.

Both institutions have changed over time. Preschools have evolved in a relatively short time to being educational institutions. With the passage of a 1994 law, preschool education became the first level of schooling (*Law on Preschools.*

No. 78 1994). The Ministry of Education now formulates national educational policy and curriculum guidelines for preschools as well as for primary schools. Children are not required to attend preschools, but according to legislation all children must have the opportunity to do so. Preschools today are intended for children under 6 years old, or until they begin primary school in the fall of the year they turn 6, whichever comes first. Most children start preschool when they are 2 years old. Approximately 96 per cent of all children ages 3–5 years, 93 per cent of 2-year-old children and 35 per cent of 1-year-old children attended preschools in 2010 (Statistics Iceland 2011).

The structure of primary schools has also evolved, and the school day is becoming longer. In 1970, special classes for 6-year-old children were established in the primary schools, and it became general practice to enroll 6-year-old children in the primary school. These classes were not compulsory, and the children attended only for an hour and a half each day. In 1991, primary school became compulsory for 6-year-olds and then the class became first grade (*Law on Compulsory Schools. No. 49* 1991). At the time, the children attended first grade half-day, either in the morning or in the afternoon. Today, children in Iceland start primary school in the fall of the year they become 6 years old. They attend first grade daily from 9am to 2pm and may attend optional after-school programmes. Gradually, the curriculum and the textbooks are becoming more demanding and more academically oriented (Einarsdottir 2003a).

This chapter will discuss transition to school from the perspectives of important stakeholders, that is, the children. Studies conducted with young children in Iceland in the last few years will be reviewed and analysed, with the aim of eliciting children's perspectives on the differences between preschool and primary school. The studies are premised on the views of childhood studies where childhood is regarded as an important and interesting period and a distinct research area. Children are viewed as strong and competent actors in their own lives, citizens with rights who are capable of holding and expressing their own opinions. An attempt is made to gain understanding of childhood and children's lives from their own perspectives. Emphasis is placed on taking children's perspectives seriously, thus allowing them to influence policy and practice (Brooker 2011; Clark & Moss 2001; Corsaro 1997; Dahlberg & Moss 2005; Jenks 2004; Mayall 2000; Qvortrup 2002; Warming 2005).

Children's perspectives on transition to school

Children are the key players in transition to school. During the last decade, the author of this chapter has conducted several studies with young children in Iceland with the aim of eliciting their perspectives on transition from preschool to primary school (Einarsdottir 2003b, 2010, 2011, 2012). The studies were conducted with preschool children in their last year of preschool and with first-grade primary school children. The theoretical foundations of the studies were an ideology of childhood studies in which childhood is viewed as an important period, contingent on culture, time and context. Furthermore, transition studies were also taken into consideration. Below, an overview of findings from these studies will be presented.

Preschool children's expectations on starting school

To investigate preschool children's views and attitudes on their transition to primary school, group interviews were conducted with 48 5- to 6-year-old preschool children in Reykjavik in May of their last year in preschool. The findings of the study (Einarsdottir 2003b) show that many of the participating children were preoccupied with the ways in which the primary school would be different from preschool, including the structure, the organisation, the size, the presence of a school bell and recess. They also saw learning the customs of the school, the school rules and how to behave in school as important parts of what they would be learning in first grade.

Many of the children had formed a view of primary school as a serious place where they would learn how to read, write and do mathematics. Everything would be bigger and more difficult there. Although they had been in preschool for some time, they did not perceive it as school. For them, first grade was real school. Although they acknowledged that they had been doing and learning many things in preschool, they believed that primary school would be much more difficult, and some did not feel that they really had been taught anything in preschool. For example, they believed that they had learned the letters of the alphabet in preschool by themselves, whereas in primary school they would be taught how to read and write.

The children described their coming transition into primary school with mixed feelings. Many of them seemed to look forward to starting school and being in new surroundings and learning new things; others were anxious about not being able to meet the school's expectations or do what they were supposed to, and some children worried about the older children and the principal. When the children talked about what they would miss about preschool, they most often mentioned that they would miss the preschool staff and the other children. They also mentioned that they would miss playing and the toys. They saw recess in primary school as something to look forward to because it was perceived to be playtime. For the children, play seemed to be a vital part of life, and they seemed to begin to realise that primary school could change that.

Preparation for primary school

A more recent study (Einarsdottir 2012) also aimed to shed further light on preschool children's perspectives about the changes they anticipated would take place when they started primary school, but it also aimed to investigate how the children regarded the preparation for primary school that took place in preschool. The participants were 32 children in the oldest preschool group in two preschools in Reykjavik. Data were gathered through individual interviews based on photos that the children took themselves in the preschool. The purpose of using the children's photographs was not to analyse the photos; instead, they were used as motivation and a basis for conversations.

The findings of the study show that the children regarded starting primary school as an important transition period and expected considerable changes in their lives when they moved from preschool to primary school. They especially mentioned that there would be more demands made on them to learn certain things in primary school, such as mathematics and reading. They also discussed their concerns that the structure of the primary school would be different from preschool, with lessons and recess but limited rest periods and play.

Most of the children said that they looked forward to starting school, and they mentioned various activities that they looked forward to doing. They discussed the formal preparation for primary school that took place in preschool, where the main emphasis was on worksheets in preparation for the subjects studied in primary school. Many of the children saw these lessons as a change from the daily routines that they were used to and thought they would benefit from them when they started primary school. Preparation also consisted of visits to the primary school where they were introduced to the buildings and routines of the school. In addition, first grade children visited the preschool and talked to the children about the primary school.

The children expected changes in their lives when they moved from preschool to primary school, and they were being prepared for these changes by the preschool, parents, older children and society as a whole. It seemed that children's definition of learning is limited to the subjects of primary school. Emphasis on play and relationships and the curriculum of preschool did not seem to have the same importance in the minds of the children.

Children's transition experiences

In order to elicit children's experiences of starting primary school and the difference between those settings after they started primary school, first grade children in two primary schools in Iceland were asked about how they perceived the differences between their early childhood setting and primary school, and what they found useful from preschool when they started primary school (Einarsdottir 2011). The children's perspectives were elicited through group interviews and children's drawings a few months after they started primary school. Forty children participated. The children's preschool teachers were co-researchers, participating in the data generation. Because the preschool teachers knew the children and their prior school context, they could easily respond to and reflect upon what the children were expressing. The interviews were a social encounter: the children recalled events and reminded each other, and together with their former preschool teachers their voices were socially co-constructed. By investigating their perspectives soon after their transition from preschool to primary school, the children were also in a position to make some comparisons.

The findings of this study indicate that the children found the main differences between preschool and primary school included the curriculum, with its greater emphasis on academics, the different teaching methods and the changes in their own status and responsibilities. The children talked about many things that they had learned in preschool, such as interpersonal relationships, manners and self-esteem. But when it came to which of these they considered useful in primary school, they talked mainly about academics and the learning of rules. Many of the children mentioned that they had practiced sitting still, being quiet and doing what they were supposed to do, and that they had become useful in school. This is an important message and an indicator of which issues are most valued in primary school. The study offers evidence that connectedness and relationships are important factors in early childhood education and in the transition to primary school. Peers and relationships seemed to be of greatest importance in the minds of most of the children when they recalled their preschool experiences.

Early experiences of school

Another study investigated the views of first grade children on the primary school curriculum and their influence on decision-making in school, and conveyed important messages from children about their experiences during their first months of primary school (Einarsdottir 2010). The study was conducted with 29 6- and 7-year-old children in one primary school. The data gathered included varied research methods, such as group interviews and children's photographs and drawings, to elicit their perspectives and opinions. The children agreed that being in primary school was very different from being in preschool, although they were not always capable of explaining the difference. In their minds, the order of the school day was stricter in the primary school. They had to do more waiting and listening, and play was allowed only during recess. According to the children's experiences, primary school education revolves around subjects. Most of the children saw reading and mathematics as the main function of the first grade curriculum. The children saw that the main role of their teachers was to teach these subjects. There were individual differences among the children in regard to their likes and dislikes in school. However, many children mentioned free time, recess and playing with other children as the most enjoyable parts of school, while reading and mathematics were singled out as the most difficult and boring parts.

The participating children did not experience democracy in school and did not find that they had influence on the school curriculum. Many of the children saw themselves as powerless, having little choice about what they did in school and limited influence on the curriculum. The teacher had the power, and they were expected to follow her. In most cases, the children accepted this situation as another fact of life. The children had attended preschool for three to four years before they attended primary school. Preschool was, for them, a place where they could play with their friends most of the time and make choices within certain limits. When they came to primary school, they seemed more or less to accept the radical changes in the curriculum and the demands made on them.

What we have learned

In the Nordic countries, almost all children have attended preschool for several years before they start primary school. However, preschools and primary schools in the Nordic countries have different histories, traditions and philosophies. The Swedish researchers Gunilla Dahlberg and Hillevi Lenz Taguchi (1994) have highlighted two different views of children predominant in preschools and primary schools. In the preschool philosophy, childhood is seen as the innocent period of a person's life where freedom and innocence are emphasised. In the primary school, on the other hand, the image of the child has been as a reproducer of culture and knowledge. Child-directed and play-oriented methods have predominated in preschools instead of teacher direction, content areas and large-group instruction experienced in the primary school (Dahlberg & Lenz Taguchi 1994). This is in harmony with the Icelandic national curriculum guidelines for preschool and primary school, which clearly represent different views on children, teaching, learning and the curriculum (Mennta- og menningarmálaráðuneytið 2011a, 2011b). The results of the four studies reviewed above indicate that Icelandic children are very much aware of the differences between the two institutions and view starting primary school as a turning point in their lives. The findings are in considerable harmony with results from other transition studies that have examined children's views on transition from preschool to primary school (Broström 2006; Corsaro & Molinari 2000a, 2000b, 2005; Dockett & Perry 2007; Eide & Winger 1994; Griebel & Niesel 2002, 2003; Loizou 2011; Peters 2010a, 2010b; Yeo & Clarke 2005).

Findings from these four Icelandic studies, taken together (Einarsdottir 2003b, 2010, 2011, 2012), reveal several patterns.

Status and responsibilities

In the minds of the children moving from preschool to primary school, they experienced a change in their social status. They were now becoming school children with more responsibilities than before. They had previously been the oldest and most respected group in preschool, but now they were the youngest in school. Now they have older children to worry about. They also have to deal with a new group of children and gaining status in that peer group.

Teaching methods

The children regarded the main change when they moved from preschool and primary school as having more demands made on them to learn specific things, such as learning how to read and do mathematics. They also found the teaching methods and the organisation of the primary school to be very different from preschool, with group instruction, well-defined lessons and recess in between.

Democracy

The children who had already started primary school reported that they found they had less influence on what they did in primary school than before. In preschool they had opportunities to choose what to do and with whom, in contrast to the primary school where the teacher was the one who had the power to make decisions, and the curriculum had restrictions.

Definitions of learning

The children who participated in these studies seem to have traditional views of what learning and teaching consist of. They seemed to connect the concepts of teaching and learning with the subjects taught in the primary school and with formal situations that were not part of preschool but a vital part of primary school. The children did not seem to connect the play and creative activities of the preschool with the concept of learning.

Missing other children and play

When the children talked about the things they would miss from preschool, they frequently mentioned other children and the preschool staff. They also said that they would miss playing and the toys. The studies with the primary school children also reflect these concerns; peers and relationships seemed to be most important, and they missed being able to spend their day playing with other children.

Preparation for primary school

The children who participated in the studies had been prepared for primary school through various transition activities. They had visited the primary school in their last year of preschool and had been introduced to the building and the organisation of the school day. Many of the preschools also had set periods once or twice a week where the children were given assignments aimed at preparing them for primary school.

Implications

In recent years, a growing interest in seeking children's views on matters that involve them and their environment has emerged. This chapter has reviewed studies conducted with preschool and primary school children in Iceland with the aim of eliciting their perspectives and experiences on transition from preschool to primary school. The findings indicate that the children had the experience, knowledge and ability to reflect on the differences between preschool and primary school and the transition to primary school. Listening to young children does not only mean hearing but also responding to what children say, and in that way have their voices influence policy and practice.

The studies reported here indicate that even before children start primary school they have a clear picture of the primary school as being fundamentally different from the preschool. It can be assumed that children's views of the differences between preschool and primary school are socially constructed and that the children formed their ideas about primary school from their social environment, including older children and their parents. Furthermore, it can be assumed that they formed their views at the preschool where some of them participated in groups as the oldest children working on preparation for school. These results are of value for preschool teachers, who might reconsider how they present the primary school. The results from the studies indicate that the children were also aware of their change of status when they started primary school and were concerned about being the youngest children in school. One way to respond to this concern could be the development of a system where an older child would take responsibility for a younger child starting school.

The studies identified disconnections for children when they move from preschool to primary school in Iceland, in spite of the common use of transition activities and preschool children's visits to the primary school. Recently, transition activities, such as those the Icelandic children had participated in, which aimed at preparing children for primary school, have been criticised. Criticism has been aimed at regarding the primary school as an unchangeable unit to which the children have to adjust and to which the preschool must deliver children who are ready. It has been pointed out that instead of focusing on the preparation of children, the primary schools have to be ready to welcome diverse groups of children and build on their prior experiences (Peters 2010b; Petriwskyj & Grieshaber 2011). Development of future transition policies has to keep the focus on continuity in children's education and build on their experiences, knowledge and skills.

References

Brooker, L. (2011) 'Taking children seriously: An alternative agenda for research?', *Journal of Early Childhood Research* 9(2): 137–149.

Broström, S. (2006) 'Children's perspectives on their childhood experiences', in J. Einarsdottir and J.T. Wagner (eds.) *Nordic Childhoods and Early Education: Philosophy, Research, Policy, and Practice in Denmark, Finland, Iceland, Norway, and Sweden* (pp. 223–256), Charlotte, NC: Information Age Publishing.

Clark, A. and Moss, P. (2001) *Listening to Young Children: The Mosaic Approach*, London: National Children's Bureau.

Corsaro, W.A. (1997) *The Sociology of Childhood*, Thousand Oaks: Pine Forge.

Corsaro, W.A. and Molinari, L. (2000a) 'Entering and observing in children's worlds: A reflection on a longitudinal ethnography of early education in Italy', in P. Christensen and A. James (eds.) *Research with Children: Perspectives and Practices* (pp. 179–200), New York: Falmer.

Corsaro, W.A. and Molinari, L. (2000b) 'Priming events and Italian children's transition from preschool to elementary school: Representation and action', *Social Psychology Quarterly* 63: 16–33.

Corsaro, W.A. and Molinari, L. (2005) *I Compagni: Understanding Children's Transition from Preschool to Elementary School*, New York: Teachers College Press.

Dahlberg, G. and Lenz Taguchi, H. (1994) *Förskola och Skola: Om Två Skilda Traditioner och om Visionen om en Mötesplats [Preschool and School: Two Different Traditions and the Vision about a Meeting Place]*, Stockholm: HLS Förlag.

Dahlberg, G. and Moss, P. (2005) *Ethics and Politics in Early Childhood Education*, London: RoutledgeFalmer.

Dockett, S. and Perry, B. (2007) *Transitions to School: Perceptions, Expectations, Experiences*, Sydney: UNSW Press.

Eide, B. and Winger, N. (1994) *'Du Gleder deg Vel til å Begynne på Skolen!' [Aren't You Looking Forward to Starting School]*, Oslo: Barnevernsakademiet.

Einarsdottir, J. (2003a) 'Charting a smooth course: Transition from playschool to primary school in Iceland', in S. Broström & J.T. Wagner (eds.) *Early Childhood Education in Five Nordic Countries: Perspectives on the Transition from Preschool to School* (pp. 101–127), Arhus: Systime/Academic.

Einarsdottir, J. (2003b) 'When the bell rings we have to go inside: Preschool children's views on the primary school', *European Early Childhood Educational Research Journal. Transitions, Themed Monograph Series* 1: 35–50.

Einarsdottir, J. (2010) 'Children's experiences of the first year of primary school', *European Early Childhood Education Research Journal* 18: 163–180.

Einarsdottir, J. (2011) 'Icelandic children's transition experiences', *Early Education and Development* 22(5): 737–756.

Einarsdottir, J. (2012) 'Þá byrjar kennarinn að láta mann læra: Leikskólabörn tjá sig um væntingar sínar og undirbúning undir grunnskólagönguna' [Then the teacher starts to let you learn: Preschool children express their expectations and preparation for primary school], *Tímarit um Menntarannsóknir* 7: 96–111.

Griebel, W. and Niesel, R. (2002) 'Co-constructing transition into kindergarten and school by children, parents and teachers', in H. Fabian & A.W. Dunlop (eds.) *Transitions in the Early Years: Debating Continuity and Progression for Children in Early Education* (pp. 64–75), London: RoutledgeFalmer.

Griebel, W. and Niesel, R. (2003) 'Successful transitions: Social competencies help pave the way into kindergarten and school', *European Early Childhood Education Research Journal. Themed Monograph Series* 1: 25–33.

Jenks, C. (2004) 'Constructing childhood sociologically', in M.J. Kehily (ed.) *An Introduction to Childhood Studies* (pp. 77–95), Berkshire, England: Open University Press.

Law on Compulsory Schools. No. 49 (1991) Reykjavik: Government Offices of Iceland.

Law on Preschools. No. 78 (1994) Reykjavik: Government Offices of Iceland.

Loizou, E. (2011) 'Empowering aspects of transition from kindergarten to first grade through children's voices', *Early Years: An International Journal of Research and Development*, 31: 43–55.

Mayall, B. (2000) 'Conversations with children: Working with generational issues', in P. Christensen and A. James (eds.) *Research with Children: Perspectives and Practices* (pp. 120–135), New York: Falmer.

Mennta- og menningarmálaráðuneytið (2011a) *Aðalnámskrá Grunnskóla* [*National Curriculum for Compulsory Schools*]. Online, available at: <http://www.menntamalaraduneyti.is/utgefid-efni/namskrar/nr/3953> (accessed June 2012).

Mennta- og menningarmálaráðuneytið (2011b) *Aðalnámskrá Leikskóla* [*National Curriculum for Preschools*]. Online, available at: http://www.menntamalaraduneyti.is/utgefid-efni/namskrar/nr/3952 (accessed June 2012).

Peters, S. (2010a) *Literature Review: Transition from Early Childhood Education to School. Report to the Ministry of Education*, Wellington: Ministry of Education.

Peters, S. (2010b) 'Shifting the lens: Re-framing the view of learners and learning during the transition from early childhood education to school in New Zealand', in D. Jindal-Snape (ed.) *Educational Transitions: Moving Stories from around the World* (pp. 68–84), New York: Routledge.

Petriwskyj, A. and Grieshaber, S. (2011) 'Critical perspectives on transition to school: Reframing the debate', in D.M. Laverick and M.R. Jalongo (eds.) *Transitions to Early Care and Education: Educating the Young Child* (pp. 75–86), New York: Springer.

Qvortrup, J. (2002) 'Sociology of childhood: Conceptual liberation of children', in F. Mouritsen and J. Qvortrup (eds.) *Childhood and Children's Culture* (pp. 43–78), Odense: University Press of Southern Denmark.

Statistics Iceland (2011) Online, available at: <http://www.hagstofa.is/Hagtolur/Mannfjoldi> (accessed 11 June 2011).

Warming, H. (2005) 'Participant observation: A way to learn about children's perspectives', in A. Clark, A.T. Kjørholt and P. Moss (eds.) *Beyond Listening: Children's Perspectives on Early Childhood Services* (pp. 51–70), Bristol: Policy Press.

Yeo, S.L. and Clarke, C. (2005) 'Starting school: A Singapore story told by children', *Australian Journal of Early Childhood* 30: 1–19.

8

WHAT NEW CHILDREN NEED TO KNOW

Children's perspectives of starting school

Kay Margetts

The importance of children contributing to the matters that concern them is increasingly being recognised. As children participate in school life, they contribute to and adopt the 'culture' of the school. By listening to and responding to the voices of children who have been directly involved in the transition to school process, valuable insights are provided. This chapter reports the perspectives of 54 children in the first year of schooling in Victoria, Australia, about what new entrant children need to know as they start school and what they think schools can do to help children starting school. Children's responses were categorised to identify emerging issues around peer relationships, school rules, general procedures, classrooms, academic skills and emotions and feelings. The ability of children to make links between what they think new entrant children need to know and what schools can do to assist new entrant children was very strong, even though children were not prompted to make these links. The playground was a key focus of children's responses, including concerns about their own safety, and raises a number of issues. The perspectives expressed in this study can be used to challenge and reconceptualise beliefs and practices about transition and adjustment to school.

Starting school

The challenges and demands of starting school have been widely documented by researchers in many countries. There is general agreement that the success of this transition to school and adaptation to the new physical, social and academic contexts is mediated on many fronts, including: child, family, school and community. From the perspectives of young children, starting school 'means learning and achievement' (Niesel & Griebel 2001: 8). It is a time when learning and education become formalised, when conformity to rules and expectations, and relationships with others, become a measure of success. Children's social and affective well-being and learning are important and can make the difference between a child progressing well or experiencing ongoing difficulties (Alexander, Entwisle & Kabbani 2001; Cowan et al. 1994; Kienig 2000; Pascall 2002; Smart et al. 2008; Taylor 1998; Wildenger et al. 2008; Wagner 2003).

Social, affective and learning competencies are supported when children's basic needs are met (Fabian 2000). From Maslow's (1970) perspective, these needs include physiological and safety needs, affective needs, recognition and esteem needs and a sense of competence – of being able both socially and intellectually. It can be argued that as children make the transition and initial adjustment to school, the meeting of these needs influences children's identity as a school child and their learning. As suggested by Fernie (1988), these initial impressions can become the standard against which future school experiences are judged.

Becoming a school child involves interpreting information and constructing understandings about school and the role of students. This includes knowing about school and responding to and taking on the behaviours and expectations of the new environment. The variation in individual development and experiences of each child means that, for some children, the new experiences encountered at school will provide minimal challenges and difficulties, while for others, the same experiences will provide heightened challenges and difficulties (Clancy, Simpson & Howard 2001; Margetts 2007).

Children's transition and adjustment to school is such a critical issue that the Australian Government Department of Education, Employment and Workplace Relations (DEEWR) with the Council of Australian Governments (COAG) (2009) has explicitly identified the importance of practices that support 'Continuity of Learning and Transitions' as a key focus in the new national early years framework – *Belonging, Being and Becoming: The Early Years Learning Framework for Australia (EYLF)*. In adopting this framework the Department of Education and Early Childhood Development (DEECD) (2009a) in the state of Victoria has introduced the *Victorian Early Years Learning and Development Framework for all Children from Birth to Eight Years (VEYLDF)* and has specifically emphasised the importance of transition to school with its comprehensive *Transition: A Positive Start to School* initiative unpinned by the recognition that '… most importantly, we know that a successful start to school is linked to future positive school outcomes, both academically and socially' (DEECD 2009b: 3).

Children's agency

Social and affective competence is vital in school and the ability to establish relationships and interact with others contributes strongly to children's well-being and learning (Missal & Hojnoski 2008). These social and affective skills are related to cooperation, assertion and self-control, and the ability to control one's emotional responses. Interpersonal skills include the ability to listen to and follow instructions, to interact with others, join existing social groups, include others, be responsible for one's own behaviour, respond appropriately to conflict and control one's feelings, such as not hitting or hurting others and not verbally abusing others (Margetts 2004, 2005). Furthermore, skills related to literacy and numeracy are also important (Bohan-Baker & Little 2004; Broström 2010; Hansen 2010).

Conformity to social rules and expectations and building 'relationships with other children is a major challenge' (Pollard 1996 cited by Fabian 2000: 6). It is likely that the school playground in particular poses enormous social challenges to children due to their limited skills for negotiating and establishing relationships (Smith 2003), and the limited adult supervision and support available. At preschool the adult:child ratio remains constant whether the child is indoors or out-of-doors. At school this is not the case and there is little supervision for children in the playground. Success in the playground can build self-esteem and confidence while the opposite may be true for those who lack social autonomy (Weare 2000). Smith (2003) devised a social skills programme to assist children develop skills for negotiating the demands of the playground. This included learning about being friends, dealing with unfriendly behaviour and aggressive behaviour, fighting or quarrelling, sharing, turn-taking, being comforted, being lonely, stealing and telling a secret.

Much of the current research about challenges facing children as they commence schooling has been obtained from parents, teachers and other adults. The importance of children contributing to the processes that affect them and the inclusion of their perspectives in research about early childhood issues is being recognised by a few researchers (Dunlop 2002), and a number have sought the perspectives of children about their experiences of starting school (Dockett & Perry 1999a, 1999b; Einarsdottir 2003; Fabian 2000; Niesel & Griebel 2001; O'Kane 2007; Peters 2000; Shepherd & Walker 2008; Skinner et al. 1998; White & Sharp 2007; Wong 2003; Yeo & Clarke 2005).

As children participate in school life they start to contribute to, and to adopt, the 'culture' of that context (Fabian 2000). The reality of the child's view may differ from that of adults (Heinzel 2000 cited in Griebel & Niesel 2000). Further differentiation of experiences and perspectives occurs through the individuality of personality and experience that each child brings to their impressions and interactions within the school. This view recognises the agency of children as co-constructors of their sociocultural environments. By listening to and analysing the 'voices' of children who have been directly involved in the transition to school process, a third dimension is added to the voices of parents and teachers.

Children who were interviewed by Peters (2000) as they commenced school, and three years later, identified difficulties with school related to misunderstandings of the language and terminologies used by teachers, the school bells (first bell, second bell) and changes in curriculum – limited time for play, not knowing 'stuff', finding 'stuff' hard and 'being right'. Similarly, children in other studies have expressed concern about the school facilities and procedures (Dockett & Perry 1999a; Yeo & Clarke 2005) and about changes in the curriculum, including limited time for play (Einarsdottir 2003; Griebel & Niesel 2000; White & Sharp 2007).

In a number of studies (Dockett & Perry 1999a, 1999b; Wong 2003; Yeo & Clarke 2005), children have noted concerns about knowing and adhering to school rules, particularly procedural or task rules or what Dockett and Perry (1999a) referred to as social adjustment or organisational adjustment rules. It is likely that children use rules (expectations) to monitor their own behaviour and 'goodness' (Skinner et al. 1998), and this provides new entrant children with a level of familiarity, comfort and predictability that influences their perceptions of being successful at school.

Concerns and challenges with friendship and relationships have been noted by children in relation to their experiences of starting school. These have included knowing and finding friends and having someone to play with (Dockett & Perry 1999a; Griebel & Niesel 2000; Peters 2000; Wong 2003; Yeo & Clarke 2005).

A range of approaches has been identified for identifying the voice of children, including the use of non-verbal methods such as painting, construction, dramatisation and narrative or storytelling (Fuhs 2000 cited in Griebel & Niesel 2000). By contrast Zinnecker (1996) and Heinzel (2000b), both cited in Griebel and Niesel (2000), recommend 'free conversation', dialogue and group discussion. Heinzel suggests that group discussion provides information about what is essentially a collective experience. Peers and peer interaction influence the expression of ideas and stimulate ideas and memories, and having a group of children reduces the dominance of the adult interviewer that would occur in one-on-one interviews.

Heinzel (2000), cited in Griebel and Niesel (2000), has raised cautions in relation to including the 'voice of children' in research. The age and maturity of children may inhibit their ability to express or say what they want; it may be difficult for adults to separate fact from fantasy; children's views may be inhibited by their desire to 'say the right thing'; and adults may manipulate or distort responses. Thus, careful analysis is required.

Research with children has thus provided valuable information about children's experiences, expectations and perceptions of starting school and in some cases has been integrated with the perspective of teachers and parents (Dockett & Perry 1999a). By placing children in the role of experts who, rather than being asked to recount their own experiences, can apply their experiences and observations to provide advice about issues affecting children commencing school, it may be possible to affirm and also extend current understandings around the transition to school.

The study

This project investigated the perspectives of children in the first year of schooling about what they believed new entrant children needed to know about starting school and what schools could do to help children starting school.

Fifty-four children in the first year of schooling (the year before Year 1) who attended three government primary schools and one private school were interviewed after attending school for seven months. This time frame was chosen as it provided children with time to become familiar with different aspects and challenges of schooling and at the same time for memories of starting school to be relatively fresh. Two schools had preschools attached (a private school and a government school) and the schools comprised families from similar socio-economic and cultural backgrounds. Schools, parents and children were informed about the project and consent was invited from and granted by each party.

Small focus group interviews were conducted with children mostly in groups of three, although there were two groups of two children and two groups of four children. The use of small focus groups has been used in previous research by Dockett and Perry (1999a), Einarsdottir (2003), Peters (2000) and Griebel and Niesel (2000) in relation to children's experiences or expectations of starting school. Interviewing children about starting school acknowledges their agency in their own schooling and enables their voices to be heard among the voices of teachers, parents and academics.

Interviews were audio recorded with school, parent and child permission. Children were asked simple questions: firstly, 'What do you think new children starting school need to know?'; then, after each child in the focus group had an opportunity to respond to the first question, the final question, 'What can schools do to help children who are starting school?' was asked, and all children in the focus groups were given opportunities to contribute ideas. These questions were chosen as it was believed that, by depersonalising the questions and creating a situation where the children were empowered to give advice, children would be able to reflect their own experiences and interpretations of school in a non-threatening way. Rephrasing and probes were used if needed and, while children's responses sometimes followed their own interests, responses were generally related to the question being asked. Wherever possible, prompting for particular responses or asking leading questions was avoided as the aim of the project was to identify, not to influence, children's perspectives. Interviewing children about starting school acknowledges their agency in their own schooling and enables their voices to be heard among the voices of teachers, parents and academics.

Audio recordings of each focus group were transcribed and analysed independently by the two interviewers to identify emerging or repetitive types of responses. Responses generally related to relationships and interactions with others, procedures, feelings about school and academic skills. Six categories were identified, relating to knowledge about: peer relationships; school rules; general procedures; classrooms; academic skills; and feelings. A smaller category, 'Other', included items not in the main categories that related to the use of outdoor equipment and sports.

Results

Children's responses to the question 'What do you think new children starting school need to know' resulted in 248 coded responses. Eighty-eight coded responses were received in response to the question 'What can schools do to help children who are starting school?'. Where an individual provided the same response more than once or referred to the same issue more than once, these were coded as only one response. Due to the strong relationship between children's perspectives about what new children need to know and what schools can do to help even though children were not prompted to do this, responses to both questions are presented simultaneously for each category as shown in Table 8.1. Children's responses to what new children commencing school need to know frequently referred to issues around peer relationships (28.2 per cent) and academic skills (27.4 per cent). However, in combination, issues around school rules, general procedures and classrooms and teachers composed 34.2 per cent of responses. When comparing the different categories of children's responses for what children need to know with how schools could help new children starting school, similar response rates occurred for peer relationships and classrooms and teachers, but there were lower proportions for academic skills and school rules. However, when responses in relation to rules, general procedures and classrooms and teachers are combined, the proportion of these responses (42.0 per cent) was considerable.

TABLE 8.1 Response categories

Categories	What children need to know	How schools can help
	Number (and percentage) of responses	Number (and percentage) of responses
Peer relationships	70 (28.2)	27 (30.7)
School rules	36 (14.5)	5 (5.7)
General procedures	26 (10.5)	23 (26.1)
Classrooms and teachers	23 (9.2)	9 (10.2)
Feelings	14 (5.7)	6 (6.8)
Academic skills	68 (27.4)	14 (15.9)
Other	11 (4.4)	4 (4.5)
Total	248	88

The following section describes responses in each of the response categories and themes within these categories illustrated by narrative responses. The responses are expressed as percentages of the broad response category, not the total responses for the study.

Peer relationships

Responses that were categorised in relation to knowledge about peer relationships are presented in Table 8.2. Many of the responses about what new children need to know included those associated with pro-social skills such as establishing friendships, knowing children's names, considering the feelings of others, sharing and taking turns. Two students also noted the importance of children being responsible for themselves – (they) *have to be responsible for themselves sometimes* – and knowing how to deal with bullying.

Knowing that finding and making new friends is difficult and part of starting school was frequently noted:

> Know that they have to um ... find new friends.
> Find it difficult to make new friends.
> They might not know if they're going to meet new friends or not.

TABLE 8.2 Knowing about peer relationships and how schools can help

Knowledge related to peer relationships	n	%	Help with relationships	n	%
Friendships, being a buddy	24	34.3	Help to meet people, give a friend	3	11.1
Knowing names	5	7.1	Tell everyone's name, list names, name badges	2	7.4
Being nice, not being mean, helping, sharing, taking turns, including others	18	25.7	How to be nice, not be rude	2	7.4
Not hurting, being gentle	15	21.4	Not to hurt, how to behave	2	7.4
Not bullying, how to deal with bullying	7	10.0	What to do if someone hurts you, how not to be a bully	11	40.7
Being responsible for oneself	1	1.4			
			Help in the yard – teacher on duty	3	11.1
			Have a buddy, a Grade 1 child to help	4	14.8
Total	70			27	

Being discerning was also noted:

> ... know who to make friends with.

Further difficulties with friendship were noted rather poignantly by one child who said:

> You can't have the same friends all the time.

And by another who commented that new children need to know that they will be mixing with unfamiliar children:

> Sit next to your friends which you don't know.

Knowing children's names was important for some children, and this appeared to assist in the establishment and cementing of friendships:

> Knowing who all their school friends are ... You need to know your school friends like if you're playing you won't call them different names you have to call them their right name.

> F: They need to know ... their friend's names.
> J: ... the other kids um, might tell their name to you and you might make friends with them once they know your name.

Interactions with peers and knowing to be nice, not mean and to be helpful were frequently noted:

> When some new kids come don't be mean to them.
> Ahh, friends and be nice.

Knowing about the playground and about turn-taking conventions was also noted:

> Don't go on the monkey bars too lots of times ... you have to wait your turn ... you have to line up.

Hurting or being hurt permeated the discussions. New children need to:

> Learn not to hurt people.
> Be gentle.

Hurting and being hurt by others appeared to be a key issue in the playground and many of the responses about what schools could do to help new children starting school related to help with knowing how not to hurt and knowing what to do when you were hurt or experienced conflict. The help of teachers and principals was recommended by children, including teachers being on yard duty:

> Teachers can help them if they get hurt.
> If you told them to stop and they kept going then you could tell (the teacher).
> If the principal takes care of the whole school no one will get hurt.
> They could write what you did bad in the book. Once Mrs … was out there … and someone kicked me in the nuts so I told the principal.

Being told or shown how to use the equipment safely was also mentioned:

> You have to show them how to do that so they don't get hurt.

During informal conversation at the end of one focus session when children were being asked to eat their lunch and hurry outside, the children asked if they could stay and talk. When probed about going outside they indicated that being in the playground was difficult because 'people fight and kids hurt'.

A range of ideas was suggested in relation to supporting friendships and interactions. It was suggested that schools could help by – *giving children friends*.

Having someone else to rely on during the start to school, whether for social or academic or other reasons, was recommended. As noted previously, this could be the teacher or principal, but it could also be an older more experienced child:

> A friend that has already been in prep … they could help, they could help you do things.

School rules

Social institutions usually have a set of clearly articulated rules for protecting members of the group and setting standards for behaviour. Schools are no exception and, as noted in Table 8.3, 36 responses related to knowing school rules, awareness of consequences, being good (not bad) and avoiding or not getting into trouble:

> Be good so … you don't get into trouble by teachers.

Children often recited rules but, as this was not the focus of the study, these separate listings of rules were not coded as separate responses.

Knowing and remembering the school rules was referred to often and difficulties doing this seemed to be accepted as a rite of passage. Almost in an off-hand way children would say, when talking about rules, *I can't remember.* As in one discussion:

TABLE 8.3 Knowing about school rules and how schools can help

Knowledge related to rules	n	%	Help with doing right thing	n	%
Knowing the rules	17	47.2	Instructions	1	20.0
Consequences of breaking rules	7	19.4			
Being good, not being bad, avoiding trouble	11	30.6	Tell us not to be naughty; tell us if doing wrong thing; tell off	4	80.0
Playing safely	1	2.8			
Total	36			5	

> L: Yep, like Bradley he doesn't know a bit of the school rules.
> E: I know cos he's new.
> L: He's new.
> E: Yeah, because he's a new boy.

Consequences of breaking rules or not 'being good' typically related to 'having to go to the office' or sitting in the 'thinking chair' as well as loss of privileges such as play:

> And you miss out on play sometimes if you get one mark, sit out in the staff room.
> I think if you be bad so many times then you'll go on the thinking chair.

The suggestions by children of ways that schools could help new entrant children in following rules and being good show that children may be confused about what constitutes appropriate and inappropriate behaviour, or that they are trying so hard to do the right thing that they want this recognised:

> … give them a reward if they've been good or not if they've been bad, they might give them punishment.
> They could tell you if you do something bad.

General procedures

Knowledge of the school and procedures for functioning within the school were referred to in 26 responses (see Table 8.4). These involved knowing what to do (actions), where to go (locations) and the timing of routines:

TABLE 8.4 Knowing about school procedures and how schools can help

Knowledge related to school procedures	n	%	Help with procedures	n	%
Actions – what to do, asking for help, lining up with partner, responding to bells, doing show and tell	12	46.2	Actions – what to do, use the toilet	13	56.5
Doing shoe laces	1	3.8			
Locations – where to go, toilet	6	23.1	Locations – where to go, where things are	4	17.4
Time – for lunch, for music, for lining up	4	15.4	Time – when to get snack, lunch	2	8.7
How it works	2	7.7	Tell us what to do before school starts	2	8.7
How it is different	1	3.8			
			Know the games	1	4.3
			Sharing Junior Council roles – so we know what is happening	1	4.3
Total	26			23	

- Knowing about what to do:

  They need to know what they need to do.
  Learning how to, um, do show and tell.

- Knowing about where to go:

  Like learning where everything is and getting used to it ... .
  When they go to school they don't know where the classrooms are. They need to know ... I was just a little prep and then I, I was bout to go into, up there because I thought that was still my classroom ... but then I had to go in there because I was wrong, and then I ... I was going with Thomas S and I just got my head muddled up. Then I thought I was going in here and then I just ... said no, no, you need to go up there.
  Playing on the right playground.

- Knowing about the time:

  R: ... and the time.
  R: ... so they know what time it's going to be lunch.

I: Yeah.

R: … or when the music is going to go.

Knowing when to apply particular procedures can be confusing, as illustrated by the following discussion between two girls (S and M) and the interviewer 'I'. There is also a suggestion that there is one way of doing things when teachers are around and one way when they are not:

S: … when the first time when I had to go to the toilet at school, like I just went by myself because I didn't know if I … had to tell the teacher.

I: Ohh.

S: So that was hard and I think it was M who told me what to do.

I: … are you meant to tell the teacher?

S: Yeah.

M: If you're in class, but if you're at playtime you can go by yourself.

S: Yeah … there's only teachers around in your classroom.

One child noted perceptively:

They … need to know how it works … and how it is going to be different things. An how it's going to start like.

A number of suggestions about how schools could help referred to procedural issues:

Tell you what to do.

They might show you where you are not allowed to play.

They could show you where things are.

Being given information before school started was also noted as a way schools could help new children starting school.

One child commented that the school could allow children to take turns being the Junior School Council (JSC) representative. Whether this was from a desire to be acknowledged by being given an important role is not known, but the sentiment that JSC reps had privileged knowledge is clearly expressed. Thus, sharing procedural matters appeared to be important and empowering to children:

Let them be a JSC rep … so they all know what it's like. They know what it's like to do it another time … they wanna know what they have to do cos otherwise if it's in the second year then they don't know they have to – they don't know what they're doing.

Classroom procedures

Another distinct set of knowledge related to classroom procedures (23) including information about the teacher, the classroom and how to behave in the classroom. However, relatively few ideas for how schools could help new children related to this category. The items in Table 8.5 are self explanatory and very close to children's own words and do not need repeating as narrative.

Feelings and emotions

Fifteen responses related to feelings and emotions that new entrant children should know about, as identified in Table 8.6. Most frequently this involved 'not feeling scared'. The responses acknowledge that being scared is a valid feeling as children start school but that schools are really not scary:

TABLE 8.5 Knowing about classrooms and teachers and how schools can help

Knowledge related to classroom	n	%	Classroom/teacher help	n	%
About teacher, teacher's name	6	26.0	Meet the teacher	1	11.1
What classroom is like	4	17.3			
Listening to teacher, doing what teacher says	5	21.7	Teachers play games	1	11.1
Procedures – being quiet, asking permission, sitting on mat, crossing legs, hands up, show and tell	8	34.7	More time for play, for shows	2	22.2
			Give rewards, compliments	5	55.6
Total	23			9	

TABLE 8.6 Knowing about feelings and how schools can help

Knowledge related to feelings	n	%	Supporting feelings	n	%
Not feeling scared	8	57.1			
Not being shy	2	14.3			
Feeling safe	2	14.3	Look after, feel safe	2	33.3
Taking risks	1	7.1			
Enjoying school	1	7.1	Do nice things, have a good time, help you feel happy	4	66.7
Total	14			6	

Not to be scared ... Because it's not scarier when you start school. Because it's easy when you get in prep.

Ways that school could help included helping children 'feel good':

They can make sure they're having a good time.
They could make sure that none of them are not sad and they're all happy.

Academic skills

Academic skills were referred to in 68 responses, including those related to learning generally and also to specific domains or learning areas (Table 8.7). Most frequently the responses related to literacy (writing, knowledge of alphabet and phonics, reading), followed by maths and numeracy, drawing or doing art, and knowing how to learn or work:

They might not know how to do maths and literacy and journal writing like that.

Suggestions on the ways that school could help children included those related to literacy and learning in general:

They could help you if you were stuck with something.
How to do hard work
Reading and sounding out letters ...

TABLE 8.7 Knowing about academic skills and learning and how schools can help

Knowledge related to academic skills	n	%	Help for academics/learning	n	%
Writing, writing own name	24	35.3	Practice writing before school starts	1	7.1
Reading	15	22.1			
Alphabet, letter sounds	6	8.9	How to sound letters, words, write	9	64.3
Knowing words	3	4.4			
Maths, numbers	10	14.7			
Drawing, doing art	4	5.9			
Knowing how to learn things, doing hard work	6	8.9	Help them learn, give easier work	4	28.6
Total	68			14	

Other

Eleven responses did not easily fit into the previously identified areas. Being older rather than younger appeared to be important and was noted twice. Issues related to the use of the monkey bars (7) and doing sport (2) were also noted, including knowing how to use the monkey bars, sharing the monkey bars and taking turns:

> Doing the monkey bars ... cos they're hard.

When asked how schools could help, responses included having soft fall under equipment, help if children get stuck on equipment and more sports.

> If someone's stuck somewhere like on top of the monkey bars they can get up but they can't get down ... the teachers can help them down.

Discussion

The responses of children to the questions 'What do you think new children starting school need to know?' and 'What can schools do to help children who are starting school?' both reflect, and add to, the voices of children, parents and teachers about starting school. Children's responses support the notion that social, affective and learning competencies are important for children as they start school. The children in this study referred to the importance of knowing about relationships and interactions with others, school rules, procedures and ways of doing things, academic skills and feelings and emotions. References about being hurt and difficulties in the playground are cause for concern and would benefit from further investigation.

Similar to the children in the study by Dockett and Perry (1999a, 1999b), knowing procedural or task rules was important to children in the current study. This included how to do things – where to go, what to do and when to do it both within the school generally and in classrooms. It appears that knowing the school rules, how to avoid trouble and the consequences of breaking rules gives children a frame of reference by which they can function independently and determine their own (and others') moral actions. Children noted that schools can help by telling children what 'gets you into trouble' or what 'being good' involves, including telling children when they have done wrong. Explicit support might assist in providing children with a greater sense of the safety and emotional well-being referred to by Pollard (1996 cited by Fabian 2000) in relation to knowing about and behaving according to rules.

Almost 30 per cent of each of the responses related to knowing about school, and how schools can help, referred to issues around peer relationships. Knowing about how to make friends and deal with interactions, including pro-social skills such as knowing people's names, helping others, sharing and personal responsibility, and the ability to deal with bullying, were frequently noted. This supports the findings of Dockett and Perry (1999a), Griebel and Niesel (2000) and Peters (2000) about the importance of friends and social interactions as children start school. Suggestions about how schools could help in this aspect indicated that explicit help was needed with, for example, gaining friends, being nice and not rude, and dealing with conflict.

Knowledge related to learning and the curriculum appeared to be important for children starting school. Similar to children's responses in the studies by Einarsdottir (2003), Griebel and Niesel (2000), Peters (2000), White and Sharp (2007), children in this study noted that work at school is hard and there is a need for more play. Knowing how to learn and knowledge related to literacy and numeracy were also noted. The strong focus by children on the importance of knowing how to write and knowing the alphabet and letter sounds, along with suggestions that teachers could help them in sounding letters and words, suggest that these skills/knowledge are a challenge to new entrant children but may also be a means of measuring one's competence as a school child. It is likely that children are not necessarily exposed to the alphabet and phonics during their preschool years and further research should investigate if the inclusion of these skills in preschool curriculum would benefit children starting school, particularly in Australia with the introduction of the Early Years Learning Framework, which explicitly focuses on developing children's literacy abilities through play-based approaches.

Frequent mention of not being hurt, or hurting, particularly in relation to the playground, suggests that children's needs for physical and emotional safety are not being sufficiently met. This is further supported by the children's suggestions that schools need to help them know what to do when they are hurt, should provide teacher assistance in the playground and should teach children how not to hurt. This reflects the recommendation by Smith (2003) that children need to be supported in developing social and emotional skills for dealing with playground contexts. As well as social skills programmes for children prior to schooling, Smith suggested that schools should review playground practices and lunchtime routines, increase playground supervision and teacher presence in the playground, and provide targeted support for shy or lonely children. There is a need for deeper investigations into these issues and the impact of increased presence of teachers in the playground for children's sense of well-being and competence.

The understandings expressed by children in this study about what new children commencing school need to know complements and adds to current notions about school transition and adjustment. Along with the close alignment of ideas about how schools can help children commencing school, there is strong evidence for the validity of children's suggestions for dealing with issues that affect new entrant children. In particular the need for more explicit assistance in matters associated with relationships, rules and procedures, and academic skills and knowledge, is noted and should be acted on by both prior to school services and primary school. It is strongly recommended that schools and preschools involve children in the early years of schooling in decision-making processes related to supporting smooth transitions to school for new entrant children and their families.

References

Alexander, K., Entwisle, D. and Kabbani, N. (2001) 'The dropout process in life course perspective: Early risk factors at home and school', *Teachers College Record* 103: 760–822.

Australian Government Department of Education, Employment and Workplace Relations with the Council of Australian Governments (2009) *Belonging, Being and Becoming: The Early Years Learning Framework for Australia*, Australia: Commonwealth of Australia.

Bohan-Baker, M. and Little. P. (2004) *The Transition to Kindergarten: A Review of Current Research and Promising Practices to Involve Families.* Harvard Family Research Project. Online, available at: <http://www.hfrp.org/publications-resources/browse-our-publications/the-transition-to-kindergarten-a-review-of-current-research-and-promising-practices-to-involve-families> (accessed June 2012).

Broström, S. (2010) 'Fiction, drawing and play in a Vygotskian perspective', in J. Hayden and A. Tuna (eds.) *Moving Forward Together: Early Childhood Programs as the Doorway to Social Cohesion. An East–West Perspective*, Cambridge: Cambridge Scholars Publishing.

Clancy, S., Simpson, L. and Howard, P. (2001) 'Mutual trust and respect', in S. Dockett and B. Perry (eds.) *Beginning School Together: Sharing Strengths* (Ch 8), Watson, ACT: Australian Early Childhood Association.

Cowan, P., Cowan, C., Shulz, M. and Henning, G. (1994) 'Prebirth to preschool family factors in children's adaptation to kindergarten', in R. Parke and S. Kellart (eds.) *Exploring Family Relationships with Other Social Contexts* (pp. 75–114), Hillsdale, NJ: Lawrence Erlbaum Associates.

Department of Education and Early Childhood Development (DEECD) (2009a) *Victorian Early Years Learning and Development Framework for All Children from Birth to Eight Years (VEYLDF).* Melbourne: Early Childhood Strategy Division of the DEECD and Victorian Curriculum and Assessment Authority.

Department of Education and Early Childhood Development (DEECD) (2009b) *Transition: A Positive Start to School. A Guide for Families, Early Childhood Services, Outside School Hours Care Services and Schools.* Melbourne: Early Childhood Strategy Division of the DEECD.

Dockett, S. and Perry, B. (1999a) 'Starting school: Perspectives from Australia'. Paper presented at the Annual Meeting of the American Educational Research Association, Montreal, 19–23 April 1999, EDRS (ED 439 811).

Dockett, S. and Perry, B. (1999b) 'Starting school: What do the children say?', *Early Child Development and Care* 159: 107–119.

Dunlop, A.W. (2002) 'Bridging early educational transition in learning through children's agency', *European Early Childhood Education Research Monograph* 1: 67–86.

Einarsdottir, J. (2003) 'When the bell rings we have to go inside: Preschool children's views on the primary school', *European Early Childhood Education Research Monograph* 1: 35–49.

Fabian, H. (2000) 'A seamless transition'. Paper presented at the 10th European Early Childhood Education Research Association Conference, London, 29 August– 1 September 2000. Online, available at: <http://extranet.edfac.unimelb.edu.au/LED/tec/> (accessed January 2012).

Fernie, D. (1988) 'Becoming a student: Messages from first settings', *Theory into Practice* 27(1): 3–10.

Griebel, W. and Niesel, R. (2000) 'The children's voice in the complex transition into kindergarten and school'. Paper presented at the 10th European Early Childhood Education Research Association Conference, London, 29 August–1 September 2000. Online, available at: <http://extranet.edfac.unimelb.edu.au/LED/tec/> (accessed June 2012).

Hansen, O.H. (2010) 'Early language and thought'. Paper presented at the 26th OMEP World Congress, Göteborg, Sweden, 11–13 August 2010.

Kienig, A. (2000) 'Transitions in early childhood'. Paper presented at the EECERA 10th European Conference on Quality in Early Childhood Education, London, 29 August – 1 September 2000.

Margetts, K. (2004) 'Identifying and supporting behaviours associated with co-operation, assertion and self-control in young children starting school', *European Early Childhood Education Research Journal* 12(2): 75–86.

Margetts, K. (2005) 'Children's adjustment to the first year of schooling: Indicators of hyperactivity, internalising and externalising behaviours', *International Journal of Transitions in Childhood* 1: 36–44.

Margetts, K. (2007) 'Preparing children for school – benefits and privileges', *Australian Journal of Early Childhood* 32: 43–50.

Maslow, A. (1970) *Motivation and Personality* (2nd edn.), New York: Harper & Row.

Missal, K. and Hojnoski, R. (2008) 'The critical nature of young children's emerging peer related social competence for transition to school', in W. Brown, S. Odom and S. McConnell (eds.) *Social Competence of Young Children: Risk, Disability and Intervention* (pp. 1117–1137), Baltimore: Paul Brookes Publishing.

Niesel, R, and Griebel, W. (2001) 'Transition to schoolchild: What children tell about school and what they teach us'. Paper presented at the 11th European Early Childhood Education Research Association Conference, Alkmaar, The Netherlands, 29 August–1 September 2001.

O'Kane, M. (2007) 'The transition to school in Ireland: What do the children say?'. Paper presented at the International Centre for Early Childhood Development and Education Conference, *The Vision for Practice: Making Quality a Reality in the Lives of Young Children*, Dublin, 8–10 February 2007.

Pascall, C. (2002) 'Foreword', in H. Fabian and W.A. Dunlop (eds.) *Transitions in the Early Years: Debating Continuity and Progression for Children in Early Education* (pp. xii–xiv), London: RoutledgeFalmer.

Peters, S. (2000) 'Multiple perspectives on continuity in early learning and the transition to school'. Paper presented at the 10th European Early Childhood Education Research Association Conference, London, 29 August–1 September 2000. Online, available at: <http://extranet.edfac.unimelb.edu.au/LED/tec/> (accessed May 2011).

Shepherd, C. and Walker, R. (2008) *Engaging Indigenous Families in Preparing Children for School*, Perth, WA: Australian Research Alliance for Children and Youth. Online, available at: <http://www.aracy.org.au/publicationDocuments/TOP_Engaging_Indigenous_Families_in_Preparing_Children_for_School_2008.pdf> (accessed July 2012).

Skinner, D., Bryant, D., Coffman, J. and Campbell, F. (1998) 'Creating risk and promise: Children's and teachers coconstruction in the cultural world of kindergarten', *The Elementary School Journal* 98(4): 297–310.

Smart, D., Sanson, A., Baxter, J., Edwards, B. and Hayes, A. (2008) *Home to School Transitions for Financially Disadvantaged Children: Final Report*. Online, available at:

<http://www.thesmithfamily.com.au/webdata/resources/files/HometoSchool_FullReportWEB.pdf> (accessed December 2011).

Smith, N. (2003) 'Transition from nursery to school playground: An intervention programme to promote emotional and social development'. Paper presented at the 13th European Early Childhood Education Research Association Conference, Glasgow, 3–6 September 2003. Online, available at: <extranet.edfac.unimelb.edu.au/LED/tec/> (accessed June 2012).

Taylor, J. (1998) *Life at Six: Life Chances and Beginning School*, Fitzroy: Brotherhood of St. Laurence.

Wagner, J. (2003) 'Introduction: International perspectives and Nordic contributions', in S. Broström and J. Wagner (eds.) *Early Childhood Education in Five Nordic Countries: Perspectives on the Transition from Preschool to School*, Arhus: Systime Academic.

Weare, K. (2000) *Promoting Mental, Emotional and Social Health: A Whole School Approach*, London: Routledge.

White, G. and Sharp, C. (2007) 'It is different because you are getting older and growing up: How children make sense of the transition to Year 1', *European Early Childhood Education Research Journal* 15(1): 87–102.

Wildenger, L., McIntyre, L., Fiese, B. and Eckert, T. (2008) Children's daily routines during kindergarten transition, *Early Childhood Education Journal* 36: 69–74.

Wong, N. (2003) 'A study of children's difficulties in transition to school in Hong Kong', *Early Child Development and Care* 173(10): 83–96.

Yeo, L. and Clarke, C. (2005) 'Starting school: A Singapore story told by children', *Australian Journal of Early Childhood* 30(3): 1–9.

PART IV

Roles, expectations and experiences of families

9

THE DEVELOPMENT OF PARENTS IN THEIR FIRST CHILD'S TRANSITION TO PRIMARY SCHOOL

Wilfried Griebel and Renate Niesel

Entry to the formal educational system – the start of primary school at age 6 years in Germany – has become an object of intense public and professional discourse and also of empirical research in different fields (Hanke & Hein 2010). Evidence about cooperation between the educational system and parents clearly shows the need for taking parents' perspectives more into account. This chapter concentrates on the meaning of transition for parents of the soon-to-be school child. It is based on transition theory modelled in the field of family developmental psychology and on findings of an explorative study (Griebel & Niesel 2009), in which developmental challenges to cope with discontinuities as well as parental coping strategies indicate changes in their lives that can be understood as development. This leads to conclusions for the cooperation between educational institutions and families. These are in line with findings from more recent research concerning: lifelong development; inter-relations between methods of transition management and the feelings of parents; and also about the participation of parents with a migration background. Some examples of practical programmes are offered.

Transition to school and a new focus: Parents in transition

Research on transition to school so far has mainly related to the challenges of children's school entry and the assessment of the resulting pressures to identify factors that influence coping with the transition to school and supportive transition management strategies (Griebel & Niesel 2011; Margetts 2002; Yeboah 2002). Evidence for better cooperation and coordination between different educational settings to ensure the progress of a child as a learner has been documented (Dunlop & Fabian 2002). Focusing on the children's perspectives in transition (Einarsdottir 2007; Einarsdottir, Dockett & Perry 2009; Griebel &

Niesel 2000; Niesel & Griebel 2001) has enhanced the understanding of what the start of school means for children. Studies have also included the parents' perspective and identified parental concerns, their ideas about school readiness and their struggles to support their children. Including parents into activities (Beelmann 2006; Margetts 2002) and communication prior to school (Pianta & Cox 1999) positively affected children's transition to the formal educational system. Research consequently demands support for parents (Beelmann 2006) as well as cooperation between the preschool institution and school with parents and the community (Clarke 2007; Jindal-Snape 2010; Margetts 2002; Pianta & Cox 1999).

German studies on cooperation between parents and schools found that institutionalised forms of communication predominate: annual parent evenings, some consulting hours and occasional collaboration of parents at school activities, such as festivals and excursions. Written information is provided through letters to parents, information sheets and reports. These contacts with parents are generally limited to the essential minimum and schools contact parents only if problems occur with the child (Walper & Roos 2001). A larger international study (Tietze, Rossbach & Grenner, 2005) has confirmed these findings and furthermore stated that other parents, who already had children in school, were an important resource of information to 'new' parents.

Overall, these studies acknowledge the important function of parents for a successful transition of their children. In consequence, more and better communication and cooperation between educational institutions and parents is needed to explore available resources. To view the transition of the first child to school as a family transition with developmental tasks for children and adults is a relatively new perspective and requires more participation of parents in managing transition more holistically. In a study on the transition of parents, perceived support (Perkonigg 1993) was related to communication between parents, nursery school and school, and to parents' participation in the cooperative transition management of the institutions.

A transition approach that includes parents' development

Researchers at the State Institute of Early Childhood Education and Research (IFP) in Munich have adopted a family developmental transition approach in a study that included the perspectives of children and their parents. Transitions – according to the IFP approach – are distinctive transformation processes for children and their families that are socially embedded and mastered by intensified learning processes of the individuals involved (in Griebel & Niesel 2011). Several theoretical concepts contribute to this constructivistic definition of transitions: the model of ecological system levels of Bronfenbrenner (1979); stress research (Lazarus 1995); the theory of critical life events of development during the lifespan (Filipp 1995); and transitions as developmental tasks in the lifespan (Havighurst 1976).

The development of adults includes learning processes and changes of attitudes resulting in enduring changes in the disposition to react to influences, to process information and to cope with problems (Brandstädter 2007). Orientation to goals and plans in life happen in interacting processes of self-regulation and individual aims as well as guided by cultural expectations, which depend on information and knowledge. Amongst these, transitions within the educational system, the working environment and the family cycle, starting with transition to parenthood, are clearly culturally and also historically embedded.

Developmental transitions involve a restructuring of one's psychological sense of self (Cowan 1991) and a shift in what Parkes (1971) described as one's assumptive world: so in life transitions one's world will be seen through 'new eyes' (Cowan 1991: 14). The agency perspective of adults' development (Brandtstädter 2007) adds to the picture of well-informed, conscious and reflective-competent parents of a school child.

Findings about parents in their child's transition to school in Bavaria/Germany

A first exploratory study was carried out in Bavaria (Griebel & Niesel 2002). Parents and nursery school pedagogues answered questionnaires concerning 162 first-born children (85 girls, 77 boys) at the end of nursery school time in March 1998. Questions referred retrospectively to transition to nursery school, to preparation for school in nursery school and at home, to the child's competences and coping strategies, to cooperation between family, nursery school and school, and to parental expectations and additional transitions within the family development (e.g. birth of siblings, employment changes, parental separation). Interviews with parents followed three and six months after the start of school. The interviews explored changes that they had experienced in their lives and strategies to cope with new demands. Additionally, 27 children were interviewed on three occasions: at the end of nursery school and at three months and six months after the beginning of school when they had got their first reports.

Developmental tasks for parents during transition from nursery school to elementary school

Analysis of the interviews revealed the many changes that parents had to deal with during the transition to being parents of a school child.

Changes at the level of the individual

The transition to school challenged mothers and fathers to adapt their identities as parents of a school child. They experienced a new sense of responsibility for securing their child's success in school. At the same time, their parental identity was affected by having less control over their child. The control was partly taken over by the teacher. School was experienced as being very powerful for their child's development. Additionally, parents had to adapt their expectations and aspirations to the child's academic success in school and to the evaluation of their further school career based on the feedback from the school.

Parents primarily pictured themselves as supporters of their child; only in hindsight did some of them realise the insecuritites they had to overcome themselves and how they gradually began to identify as being parents of a school child; included was a feeling of membership in the group of school parents.

Changes at the level of relationships

Parents had to restructure some important relationships. To begin with, parents had to deal with feelings of loss that emerged with regard to relations with nursery school professionals and other nursery school parents, as well as with friends of their children. In terms of the relationship to the school child, a growing independence had to be acknowledged. In respect to the role of a school child's parent, new expectations arose, such as monitoring homework and successfully motivating the child for school. There was a sense too that the parental partners had to renegotiate their distribution of these tasks. For parents, teachers were the central people to whom they had to cede responsibility and control and with whom they had to build up trust. New relationships developed within the group of other school parents; sometimes competition occurred among parents in terms of comparing the respective child's performance and success in school. For parents, this is an adaptation to a new norm: the assessment function of school.

Changes at the level of context

Parents, mainly mothers, had to integrate the demands of the different social systems: family, school and employment. Parents reported that the daily, weekly and yearly routines were massively influenced by school schedules and demands. They had to find either institutional solutions (e.g. day care centres during school holidays) or use social networks such as grandparents to ensure the care of their child through the course of a year. The transition of becoming the parent of a school child became more complicated if additional familial transitions occurred, such as the birth of a baby, starting a new job or if parents separated.

Coping strategies of parents in the transition to school

Parents reported how they coped with transition individually as well as within their partner relationship. Their behaviours as well as their feelings were looked upon as coping strategies. According to Lazarus and Folkman (1987), the function of coping is problem-solving and the regulation of emotional distress. Before transition, parents preferred to seek information about possible future schools from other parents. They usually did not feel fully satisfied with information offered by nursery schools and schools, and many of them preferred to consult their social networks.

Parents also put an effort into arranging for their child to be in the same class as children they already knew. This was understood as striving for social continuity for their child, but also for themselves because they then would already know some of the parents in the new class. This strategy promised to reduce the stress of change.

After the children had started school, parents were interested in information about the school day, which they tried to acquire from their children, and showed a need for orientation and control. Performance in school and comparison of performance were issues that indicated adaptation to a new institutional norm: achievement, assessment and selection. Mothers and some fathers tried to ensure that their child made a good impression at school by intensely controlling and supporting homework. They reported doing this as a support for their children – but it seemed very often that they chose this strategy in order to deal with their own fears about complying with new norms and a potential loss of status of their child in school and their success as parents.

Parents of new school children showed a tendency in the beginning to change their educational style: they put less emphasis on the child's autonomy than they did in nursery school but instead emphasised traditional values such as obedience, adaptation, punctuality and willingness to achieve predefined aims. This parental behaviour appeared not to be guided by actual information and exchange with the school, but seemed to be an action that aimed at reducing their own insecurity – which often created conflicts with their child.

Almost all parents and children reported that they had a very good impression of the first elementary teacher. The feeling of being lucky with that teacher promoted a positive feeling of security and trust in parents who felt that they had to transfer a huge part of parental responsibility concerning the future of their child. This positive attitude towards the challenges connected with transition to school can be seen as a promising coping strategy.

Discussion

Parents clearly faced discontinuities as challenges at the indivdual, the interactional and the contextual levels. As the parental attempts to cope show, becoming a parent of a school child is a transition process that begins long before their child's enrolment in school and continues after school entry. Parental coping included active problem-solving behaviour patterns, such as seeking information and structuring the day, week and year to care for their child after school, as well as emotion-regulating ways of coping. Obviously their coping efforts strongly depended on the kind of information and support that was offered by school. They accepted the new system of influence and adapted their personal goals in relation to school; they restructured their feeling of self and started to see being parents of a school child with new eyes; and they changed their disposition, attitudes and behaviours in learning to be a parent of a school child. So this conscious and reflexive transition can be viewed as a developmental step in their adult lives. To be successful and gain from a developmental step is an essential motive in life activity and seems a bit more than a mere cost–benefit analysis (Brandtstädter 2007).

For the children's successful transition, well-being has been proposed to be an important criterion (Bulkeley & Fabian 2006; Fabian 2002). Successful transitions have been found to correlate with success throughout primary school (Margetts 2002). As an analogy to that, the well-being of parents could be considered to be a criterion for a successful transition to becoming the parent of a school child too, and that they show competent school-parent attitudes and behaviour.

The following studies deepened the knowledge about parents' position

A more recent study based on the IFP transition approach (Reichmann 2010) on 118 parents' experiences and their reflections on becoming the parent of a school child replicated some of the findings from the IFP pilot study. Strong emotions on the parents' side, including grief about losses on the one hand and pride and curiosity about the new on the other, were identified; reflections of their own history as school-beginners and of their function as moderating their child's transition were also prominent. Parents emphasised their child's well-being more than their own. They were concerned about social relations in the new class and liked the new teacher too, and in the end they were content with their child's successful transition.

The study sheds some light on the influence of transition management. An aim of the study was a comparison with an intervention group where an advanced buddy system among the children had been established: older school children received a pedagogical intervention on how to help school beginners. In the intervention group, not only did the children have a better transition, but also their parents: they felt less stress and insecurity, they felt better informed about what was going on in school and they relied less on pre-training of academic skills at home to prepare their children and less on controlling their child in school. The closer the contact between them and nursery school and school, and the more detailed the feedback on their children's development had been, the less insecure the parents felt.

The importance of communication with and participation of parents during the transition to school is underlined by results from another recent study in Germany about co-working of nursery school and school with 204 parents from a migrant background (Russian and Turkish speaking) (Pfaller-Rott 2010). Migrant parents wanted to become actively involved in planning, carrying out and evaluating transition activities and made a lot of proposals that would help them, such as an ethos in school that is friendly to them and their various backgrounds, information in their own languages, use of interpreters, organisation of parents' evenings and of talks that fits with their working hours and with the need to take care of their younger children, and a kind of dialogical cooperation with teachers in nursery school and school.

At the IFP, a new study started in 2010 to investigate the support that parents experience as a result of the cooperation between nursery school and school and with them (parents) during the transition phase. Personal contact with the school and being kept informed about the transition procedures and their children's transition is expected to be the critical factor to ease the transition for the parents themselves. Seven hundred and twenty parents with a first or second child starting school in Germany were interviewed by telephone shortly before the first class of elementary school started. Topics were: the parents' perspective on the way in which cooperation between nursery school and school was managed with respect to parents' transition; participation in cooperative transition management and the support that they felt they received; and their own activities and their own experience in transition. Preliminary quantitative analyses show that most parents (98 per cent) reflected on their changing status to becoming a mother/father of a school child even before school commenced, and thought that this transition would bring about changes in their own lives (78 per cent). They imagined that not only the child but also they themselves would have to learn new things.

Parents felt supported by receiving information about 1) the organisation of school (classes, materials, enrolment, after-school care), 2) pedagogical issues (special activities for children in their last year before school, preparation for school that parents could give, parental support of homework, school curriculum), 3) expectations that schools have in respect of new children, and 4) meeting the new teacher before school starts. They also felt supported by meeting the head of the school or other parents that had school children already, and seeing and exploring the new school. Parents with a second child starting school felt much better informed about the expectation of schools.

Conclusions

The quality of participation grows if parents become integrated in a trustful, appreciative and respecting way and in partnership, if the needs of the individual child and parent are acknowledged and if parents feel space for their own emotions about transition and a new role. Thus parents are agents of their own transition process and positive encounters with nursery school and school will help them.

To view coping with transition as the development of parents is relatively new and implies consequences for cooperation between education institutes and families. Studies concerning the involvement of parents show that parents struggle to establish an educational partnership with school. Success will depend on a transition management that explicitly makes offers to parents to participate and contribute (Dockett & Perry 2004a, 2004b; Westcott et al. 2003).

The psychological model of transition for children *and* parents is gaining acceptance. Parents as stakeholders and adults in development are explicitly included in the co-construction (Valsiner 1994) of the transition from nursery school to elementary school.

There is another question to be taken into consideration – the problems that children with a linguistic–cultural minority status have during educational transitions. This is not only a problem in Germany (Die Beauftragte der Bundesregierung für Migration, Flüchtlinge und Integration 2012). On an international level, the importance of language and culture of children coming to school is in line with ideas of Dahlberg and Lenz Taguchi (1994) about values and notions in social contexts that impact the transition to formal schooling, as well as with findings of Margetts (1997, 2003) that language spoken at home has an impact on transition to school and that transition is easier when children are familiar with the school situation. From these examples of studies it seems evident that it is important to consider the possible increased complexity of the transition for children and their parents from a migrant background or with a language other than the national mainstream school language. It is in this context that two European projects intend to strengthen parents' participation in managing educational transitions for their children with support from voluntary transition counsellors (http://www.project-transition.eu/) and to ease the way by training teachers for transition management together with children and their parents in a way that is sensitive to interculturality and multi-language acquisition (www.tram-project.eu).

The chance to recognise transition developmental tasks and to deal with them appropriately depends on the parents' various life circumstances as well as on their own past experiences with school. Their social and cultural backgrounds may influence their attitudes towards educational institutions and competences (Dockett et al. 2011) and attitudes that have been labelled as 'close to education' or 'distant from education'. In comparison, international findings on diversity of family backgrounds and on impact of family factors on school success suggest that the question should be asked the other way around: to what extent do school and nursery school approach parents' different life circumstances and needs and may then be called 'close-to-family' educational institutions?

References

Beelmann, W. (2006) *Normative Übergänge im Kindesalter. Anpassungsprozesse beim Eintritt in den Kindergarten, in die Grundschule und in die weiterführende Schule*, Hamburg: Dr. Kovač.

Brandstädter, J. (2007) 'Entwicklungspsychologie der Lebensspanne: Leitvorstellungen und paradigmatische Orientierungen', in J. Brandstädter and U. Lindenberger (eds.) *Entwicklungspsychologie der Lebensspanne*, Stuttgart: Kohlhammer.

Bronfenbrenner, U. (1979) 'The ecology of human development', *Annals of Child Development*, Cambridge, MA: Harvard University Press.

Bulkeley, J. and Fabian, H. (2006) 'Well-being and belonging during early educational transitions', *International Journal of Transitions in Childhood* 2: 18–30.

Clarke, C. (2007) 'Parent involvement in the transition to school', in A.W. Dunlop and H. Fabian (eds.) *Informing Transitions in the Early Years*, Maidenhead, UK: Open University Press.

Cowan, P. (1991) 'Individual and family life transitions: A proposal for a new definition', in P. Cowan and E.M. Hetherington (eds.) *Family Transitions: Advances in Family Research*, Hillsdale, NJ: Lawrence Erlbaum Associates.

Dahlberg, G. and Lenz Taguchi, H. (1994) 'Förskola och skola – om två skilda traditioner och om visionen om en mötesplats', Särtryck no. SOU1992: 45, bilaga 3, Stockholm: HLS Förlag.

Die Beauftragte der Bundesregierung für Migration, Flüchtlinge und Integration (2012) *9. Bericht der Beauftragtren der Bundesregierung für Migration, Flüchtlinge und Integration über die Lage der Ausländer und Ausländerinnen in Deutschland*, Berlin. Online, available at: <http://www.bundesregierung.de/Content/DE/_Anlagen/IB/2012-06-27-neunter-lagebericht.pdf?__blob=publicationFile&v=1> (accessed 19 July 2012).

Dockett, S. and Perry, B. (2004a) 'Starting school: Perspectives of Australian children, parents and educators', *Journal of Early Childhood Research* 2: 171–189.

Dockett, S. and Perry, B. (2004b) 'What makes a successful transition to school? Views of Australian parents and teachers', *International Journal for Early Years Education* 12: 217–230.

Dockett, S., Perry, B., Learney, E., Hampshire, A. Mason, J. and Schmied, V. (2011) *Facilitating Children's Transition to School from Families with Complex Support Needs*, Albury, Australia: Research Institute for Professional Practice, Learning and Education, Charles Stuart University. Online, available at: <http://www.csu.edu.au/__data/assets/pdf_file/0009/154899/Facilitating-Childrens-Trans-School.pdf> (accessed 25 May 2012).

Dunlop, A.W. and Fabian, H. (2002) 'Conclusions: Debating transitions, continuity and progression in the early years', in H. Fabian and A.W. Dunlop (eds.) *Transitions in the Early Years*, London: RoutledgeFalmer.

Einarsdottir, J. (2007) 'Childrens' voices on the transition from preschool to primary school', in A.W. Dunlop and H. Fabian (eds.) *Informing Transitions in the Early Years*, Maidenhead, UK: Open University Press, McGraw-Hill Education.

Einarsdottir, J., Dockett, S. and Perry, B. (2009) 'Making meaning: Children's perspectives expressed through drawings', *Early Child Development and Care* 179: 217–232.

Fabian, H. (2002) *Children Starting School*, London: David Fulton.

Filipp, H.S. (1995) 'Ein allgemeines Modell für die Analyse kritischer Lebensereignisse', in H.S. Filipp (ed.) *Kritische Lebensereignisse* (3rd edn.), Weinheim: Beltz.

Griebel, W. and Niesel, R. (2000) 'The children's voice in the complex transition into kindergarten and school'. Paper presented at 10th European Early Childhood Research Associaion Conference on Quality in Early Childhood Education, London, 29 August–1 September 2000. Online, available at: <http://extranet.edfac.unimelb.edu.au/LED/tec/ftp.shtml> (accessed 25 May 2012).

Griebel, W. and Niesel, R. (2002) 'Co-constructing transition into kindergarten and school by children, parents and teachers', in H. Fabian and A.W. Dunlop (eds.) *Transitions in the Early Years*, London: RoutledgeFalmer.

Griebel, W. and Niesel, R. (2009) 'A developmental psychology perspective in Germany: Co-construction of transitions between family and education system by the child, parents and pedagogues', *Early Years* 29: 59–68.

Griebel, W. and Niesel, R. (2011) *Übergänge verstehen und begleiten*, Berlin: Cornelsen Scriptor.

Hanke, P. and Hein, A.K. (2010) 'Der Übergang zur Grundschule als Forschungsthema', in A. Diller, H.R. Leu and T. Rauschenbach (eds.) *Wie viel Schule verträgt der Kindergarten?*, München: Verlag DJI.

Havighurst, R.J. (1976) *Developmental Task and Education*, New York: McKay.

Jindal-Snape, D. (ed.) (2010) *Educational Transitions: Moving Stories from around the World*, New York: Routledge.

Lazarus, R.S. (1995) 'Stress und Stressbewältigung – ein Paradigma', in H.S. Filipp (ed.) *Kritische Lebensereignisse* (3rd edn.), Beltz: Weinheim.

Lazarus, R.S. and Folkman, S. (1987) 'Transactional theory and research on emotions and coping', *European Journal of Personality* 1: 141–170.

Margetts, K. (1997) 'Factors impacting on children's adjustment to the first year of primary school', *Set Research Information for Teachers* 2: 1–4.

Margetts, K. (2002) 'Planning transition programmes', in H. Fabian and A.W. Dunlop (eds.) *Transitions in the Early Years*, London: RoutledgeFalmer.

Margetts, K. (2003) 'Children bring more to school than their backpacks: Starting school down under', *European Early Childhood Education Research Monograph Series* 1: 5–14.

Niesel, R. and Griebel, W. (2001) 'Transition to school child: What children tell us about school and what they teach us'. Paper presented at 11th European Early Childhood Research Association Conference on Quality in Early Childhood Education, Alkmaar, The Netherlands, 29 August–1 September 2001. Online, available at: <http://extranet.edfac.unimelb.edu.au/LED/tec/ftp.shtml#griebelniesel4#> (accessed 25 May 2012).

Parkes, C.M. (1971) 'Psycho-social transitions: A field for study', *Social Science and Medicine* 5: 101–115.

Perkonigg, A. (1993) 'Soziale Unterstützung und Belastungsverarbeitung: Ein Modell zur Verknüpfung der Konzepte und Analyse von Unterstützungsprozessen', in A-R. Laireiter (ed.) *Soziales Netzwerk und Soziale Unterstützung*, Bern: Hans Huber.

Pfaller-Rott, M. (2010) *Migrationsspezifische Elternarbeit beim Transitionsprozess vom Elementar- zum Primarbereich*, Berlin: WVB.

Pianta, R.C. and Cox, M.J. (1999) *The Transition to Kindergarten*, Baltimore: Paul H. Brookes.

Reichmann, E. (2010) *Übergänge vom Kindergarten in die Grundschule unter Berücksichtigung kooperativer Lernformen*, Baltmannsweiler: Schneider Verlag Hohengehren.

Tietze, W., Rossbach, H-G. and Grenner, K. (2005) *Kinder von 4 bis 8 Jahren. Zur Qualität der Erziehung und Bildung in Kindergarten, Grundschule und Familie*, Weinheim: Beltz.

Valsiner, J. (1994) 'Culture and human development: A co-constructionist perspective', *Annals of Theoretical Psychology* 10: 247–298.

Walper, S. and Roos, J. (2001) 'Die Einschulung als Herausforderung und Chance für die Familie', in G. Faust-Siehl and A. Speck-Hamdan (eds.) *Schulanfang ohne Umwege*, Frankfurt: Grundschulverband.

Westcott, K., Perry, B., Jones, K. and Dockett, S. (2003) 'Parents' transition to school', *Journal of Australian Research in Early Childhood Education* 10: 26–38.

Yeboah, D.A. (2002) 'Enhancing transition from early childhood phase to primary education: Evidence from the research literature', *Early Years* 22: 51–68.

10

FAMILIES AND THE TRANSITION TO SCHOOL

Sue Dockett and Bob Perry

One of the consistent contexts for children as they start school is the family. Drawing on a base of bio-ecological theory, this chapter examines the role of families as children start school and the impact that transition to school has on families, as well as children. It draws on recent investigations of family experiences as children start school to explore the interactions of family and school contexts and to examine these as times of opportunity, aspiration, expectation and entitlement.

Introduction

Transition to school is a milestone in the lives of children and families. It is a process that occurs over time as children engage in a range of experiences that promote their learning, development and well-being.

While a great deal of research has emphasised the changes encountered and managed by children as they start school (Broström 2005; Einarsdottir 2010), a number of researchers has also explored the transition to school as a time of change for families (Griebel & Niesel 2009; Langford 2010). This research notes the changes encountered by families as they work to build new relationships with schools and teachers, construct identities as parents of school children and balance the areas of family life, school and work. Drawing on data from a recent investigation of the experiences of families as their children start school, this chapter explores the ways in which transition to school can be conceptualised as a time when families are afforded opportunities, forge aspirations, manage expectations and access entitlements.

The theoretical underpinnings of this chapter are drawn from Bronfenbrenner's bio-ecological model (Bronfenbrenner & Morris 2006), which emphasises the unique attributes that individuals bring to a given situation, the ways in which contexts influence the nature of interactions and the importance of interactions over time. In particular, proximal processes – regularly occurring interactions between children and others, ideas and objects – are considered to underpin development (Bronfenbrenner & Morris 2006). As children start school, they – and their families – participate in different ways with a range of others, including teachers and peers who influence children's development and learning. An advantage of adopting the bio-ecological model is that it promotes focus not only on the children and their interactions at times of transition, but also on the adults who are involved and the contexts in which the transitions occur.

Family contexts and the transition to school

Families and communities are social contexts that shape children's experiences and development, including the transition to school. At the community level, cohesiveness, stability and heterogeneity influence the resources (social, cultural and environmental) available for children and families during the transition to school (Nettles, Caughy & O'Campo 2008). Family habitus (Bourdieu 1997) incorporates family traditions, dispositions and expectations, often framed around family stories or experiences of education. Views of family members contribute to the family habitus and to both child and family engagement in education. In addition, the nature of the home learning environment is reported as a strong predictor of educational and behavioural outcomes for children well into the primary years (Siraj-Blatchford 2010).

Families engage in education in many ways, including helping children with homework, discussing school at home, volunteering at school and participating in school committees and programmes (Hoover-Dempsey et al. 2005). Where such involvement is supported by positive relationships between families and schools, educational outcomes are enhanced (Henderson & Mapp 2002). Such relationships are based on family commitment to education as well as positive attitudes, beliefs and perceptions within school communities about family engagement (Barnes et al. 2006).

Family changes as children start school

The transition to school involves major changes and requires adjustment at all levels as children and families respond to changing sets of demands (Dockett & Perry 2007). Families provide support for their children at transition, but they also experience a transition themselves (Griebel & Niesel 2009). Individual changes are noted as parents become 'parents of a school student' and negotiate the associated responsibilities and expectations. The transition to school is also marked by changes in relationships – for parents as well as children. Some relationships are lost and others generated as children and families leave early childhood education settings and move to school, and as different children and families become associated with different schools (Langford 2010; Peters 2003). Relationships between parents and teachers are important features in children's educational success, and much effort is expended by many parents in developing appropriate communication strategies and approaches to support their children at school (Barton et al. 2004; Hamre & Pianta 2001). Within families, relationships change as children seek greater autonomy and parents respond to the role of other significant adults in the lives of their children (Walker & McPhee 2011). At the contextual level, families work to integrate family life, work responsibilities and school.

Reconceptualising transition to school

Recent research has highlighted the importance of school, family and community factors in promoting a positive start to school (Dockett & Perry 2009). This view is compatible with bio-ecological understandings of transition, which consider the interactions of people, processes and contexts over time.

This view also underpins the development of a recent *Transition to School: Position Statement* (Educational Transitions and Change (ETC) Research Group 2011), which reconceptualises transition to school in ways that recognise children's prior experience and learning as they come to school; the strengths and competencies of all involved in the transition to school; the significance of partnerships at this time; and the importance of critical reflection on assumptions underpinning transition to school policies and practices and the ways in which they are enacted.

The position statement draws on a range of recent research to characterise transition to school in terms of opportunities, aspirations, expectations and entitlements for all involved – children, families, educators, school organisations and communities. It urges all involved in transition to school to recognise the potential of this time to promote positive, ongoing engagement with school. In relation to families, the following are identified:

1. Transition to school provides **opportunities** for families to:
   - collaborate with a range of others in ways that strengthen and support each child's ongoing learning and development;
   - reflect on children's attainments and share responsibilities for future achievements;
   - establish and maintain positive, respectful collaboration between home and school contexts that sets a pattern for ongoing interaction; and
   - build links for their children between prior-to-school and school experiences.

2. Families **aspire** to:
   - positive educational outcomes for their children;
   - continuity between the settings – at times of transition and beyond;

- children being happy and successful at school, to have friends and be respected and recognised as an individual within the various groups of which they are members; and
- contribute to their children's education through the development of trusting, respectful and reciprocal relationships.

3. Families **expect** that:
   - their knowledge of their children will be respected at school and that educators will draw on this, as well as their own expertise and that of other professionals, to create the best possible learning environments for their children;
   - they will contribute to their children's education;
   - children's safety and well-being will be central features in decisions about educational provision;
   - schools will recognise the strengths that their children bring, and be responsive to their diverse learning needs; and
   - they will be advocates for their children, and will be supported in this by the advocacy of teachers and other professionals.

4. Families are **entitled** to be:
   - confident that their children will have access to education that promotes equity and excellence and that attends to the well-being of all children; and
   - respected as partners in their children's education.

The remainder of this chapter examines the experiences of one family during the transition to school and analyses the ways in which this point in time afforded opportunities, promoted aspirations, generated expectations and identified entitlements. It also identifies instances where the potential for ongoing positive engagement among and between the participants was not met and discusses the consequences for those involved. Data reported were generated through conversational interviews with parents as part of an investigation of the experiences of families as their children started school (Dockett et al. 2011).

The Davies family

Teagan, Anthony and their three children, Chris (7 years), Danny (6 years) and Holly (1 year) [not their real names], lived in an outer metropolitan area characterised by high levels of socio-economic disadvantage. Anthony worked long hours as a truck driver. His income supported the family as well as providing child support for three other children from a previous relationship. Teagan managed the household, including the very limited financial resources, and made many of the family decisions. The family had accessed a caseworker and support from various organisations after Danny had been identified at preschool as having challenging behaviour. Much of the assistance involved financial support, although parenting support was also provided. Teagan participated in six conversational interviews with researchers over a period of 16 months, encompassing the year before Danny started school and into his first year of school. All interviews took place in the family home. In addition, researchers held conversations with Danny and his first-year school teacher, Adele.

Danny had been eligible to start school at age 5, but concerns about his behaviour and his ability to manage the more formal structure of school had resulted in the decision for him to spend another year attending preschool, attending five full days each week. Teagan expected Danny's preschool experience to help prepare him for school and establish some of the friendships that would support him at school. She was eager for Danny to have a positive start to school, do well at school and complete the final (HSC) matriculation exam:

> I'd be proud of my kids for doing the HSC because it's something I never did, neither did Anthony, so we push them to do the best they can.

With limited financial resources, the case worker organised for assistance to meet the preschool fees. One of Teagan's responses to the financial constraints experienced by the family was to plan well ahead. In the lead-up to her older son (Chris) starting school, Teagan had visited several local schools in order to determine which would provide the best environment for her children. In explaining her choice, she noted

> As soon as I walked into that school, I liked it … this one is all open, they've got the biggest playground in the world … their classes are small, they don't have that many children.

In addition, well before the school year commenced, she explained her approach:

> We sort of like to plan ahead because then we know what we've got to save for … I try to be organised … I sort of have to try and get things out of the way while I can. Like think about Danny going to school and stuff like that.

Teagan had established a collaborative relationship with the preschool teacher, and together they had promoted consistency in responding to Danny's behaviour. For example, both in preschool and at home, a reward system operated where positive behaviour earned Danny specific rewards at the end of each week. For a time, at least, this seemed to work well.

Teagan initiated contact with the school Danny would attend, indicating that his behaviour may cause some problems. She expected the school to acknowledge her expertise as a parent and reported this to be the case, as the school 'felt nice and open and it was helpful'. She also expected the school to make appropriate provision for Danny, particularly as 'they've been told he might need extra help, things like that, and they've agreed to it all'. In particular, Teagan noted:

> I've already spoken to them ... I think they're ready ... I think it makes it easier because we've had them coming, we've had Ruby (caseworker) helping us and that, and the preschool. I think it's easier for the primary school if they know there's a problem with your child ... and they have a lot more resources as well that I couldn't probably get into because they are teachers.

As a result of Teagan's initial contact, the school sent a guidance officer (teacher with background and experience in school counselling) to visit the preschool and observe Danny. Teagan only became aware of this after the event when Danny told her:

> Yeah, I only knew about the first time ... But the second time that she went I didn't even know she'd been ...

Teagan's only opportunity to talk with the guidance office was at the school orientation day, where: 'She didn't really say a lot though, she just said they would sort of be keeping an eye on him and seeing what happens ... I can't remember her name. I only met her the once.'

Describing the support Danny would have at school to help with managing his behaviour, Teagan explained:

> I'm not sure. I know he'll have a buddy from one of the older classes, like from 6th class or something. Yeah, I think that's pretty much it ... [the guidance officer] will probably, from what I gathered, she's going to let him sort of do it himself for a couple of weeks to see how he fits in. Then she'll have a conference with the teacher and see how he's going. And if all is going fine, she'll leave it for the rest of the term. If he's having any troubles though we'll have a meeting ...

Despite not knowing the nature of support available for Danny, in conversations before he started school Teagan seemed cautiously optimistic about Danny's transition to school. She commented: 'I think he'll be all right at school, probably the first term. Everything is still new; they do lots of different things. But after that, we'll wait and see.' She planned to spend some time at the school: 'I can actually go [to the school] one morning to Chris's class and one morning to Danny's class.'

Danny's experiences at school started with some challenges when, during the orientation programme, 'he got into a fight ... there was a bit of a punch up' and, in the first week of school, 'he mucked up … he was put on a level which means for two weeks there's no playing at recess or lunch'. As a consequence, Teagan had spent some time talking with the school principal. By the time of the last meeting with researchers, she had also had an interview with Danny's teacher. She found this helpful:

> because they can say things … You know how you can say something but you can't actually write it down how you want to say it. It makes it a lot easier. I think it's a bit more personal too, to be able to get on with the teacher.

Teagan indicated that she was keen to have regular, informal conversations with Danny's teacher, but indicated that the teacher 'always seems to be in a hurry though, like she needs to go out for a jog or something'. Adele, the teacher, seemed unaware of this, suggesting that:

> I think when she realised that he was going well she was happy. We did communicate at the end of the day … she's very good, she's very supportive in that way so that worked out well.

Indeed, Adele attributed Danny's challenging behaviour to being 'bored at preschool' and indicated that now he was at school and undertaking more challenging activities, his behaviour was not an issue. She 'did not know what was happening at home' but indicated that Danny 'was fine at school'.

After Danny had been at school for several months, Teagan's position was that 'I don't really have much to do with the school … I mean I don't go to … I'm not on the PTA [parent–teacher association] or … I wouldn't work in the canteen, no'. Nevertheless, she remained committed to helping Danny, but was not sure what was happening:

> [the guidance officer] spends time with him each week … I had to sign another thing for funding, for another five weeks, but that was a while ago and I think the five weeks are going to be up again soon … I haven't actually heard from her … so I have to go and see them about that and see how much time she is spending with him and what she is actually doing with him … anything that is going to help, as long as I understand what's going on.

By the time of the last meeting with Teagan, Danny seemed to have made a positive transition to school. There had been no major behavioural incidents for several months, and Adele described him as 'one of the smartest kids in the class'. Both Adele and Teagan mentioned a girl in his class who 'picked on him', sometimes in an aggressive manner, and both indicated that Danny had resisted retaliating. This was considered evidence of his changed approach to school.

Teagan maintained contact with the teacher through quick comments most afternoons, but did not seek out ways to be more actively involved in the school. She had no further contact with the guidance officer and, after a while, assumed that she was no longer working with Danny. Teagan took this as a sign that he was coping well at school. Her summary of Danny's transition to school was that:

> I was anxious about his behaviour, how he would go at school … just how he'd behave because different situations that happen at school … [but] he couldn't wait to get to school … I think he'd had enough [of preschool] … I think school is better … I mean, at preschool you can only learn so much. School is forever something new, something else to learn … I am stoked. He got a really good report, so yeah, really happy.

Discussion

The elements of the *Transition to School: Position Statement* (ETC 2011) – opportunities, aspirations, expectations and entitlements – are reflected in the experiences of Danny and his family as they started school. Danny's transition to school opened up a range of opportunities for communication and collaboration between the family, caseworker, preschool and school. Similar opportunities have been discussed by Langford (2010). Teagan indicated her willingness to be a part of this communication, through her interactions with the preschool and the school. She initiated communication with the school as a strategy to access support for Danny and provided the link between the preschool teacher, school, caseworker and family. However, she was not always included as a key contributor. For example, the guidance officer from the school communicated with the preschool teacher and the teacher at school yet did not include Teagan in these conversations. Ruby, the caseworker, had regular communication with Teagan, but not with the preschool or school. While there were many opportunities for collaboration focused on developing consistent and supportive strategies to assist Danny's transition, only some of these were embraced.

Opportunities to promote Teagan's ongoing engagement with school were neither identified nor grasped, and her original intention to spend time volunteering her support in her children's classrooms did not eventuate. While she did not indicate it explicitly, there was a sense in Teagan's latter conversations that the school did not really take her concerns about Danny seriously. Despite this, she remained committed to supporting Danny by ensuring that he attended school regularly and completed homework. Her aspirations for Danny continued to be based on him completing school and accessing the best education possible.

Teagan took the initiative in contacting the school to share her understanding of, and concerns for, Danny. She expected that her knowledge of her son would be respected and that staff at the school would respond to her concerns. This reflects the situation where all of the players in transition to school have expectations about what might happen and how it might happen (ETC 2011). There was evidence that this might be the case when the guidance officer visited the preschool to observe Danny. However, no contact was made with Teagan after the observations and she had no sense of how the information gleaned from these observations would be used to support Danny. Indeed, she only discovered that the guidance officer had been to visit the preschool from Danny and suggested that he had adapted his behaviour because he knew he was being observed. This phenomenon has also been noted by Barton et al. (2004).

Teagan had developed a collaborative relationship with the preschool teacher and had worked with her to develop consistent strategies across home and preschool. Danny's school teacher did not indicate that this was a necessary part of her role. She was pleased that Danny seemed to have settled into school and indicated that his behavioural issues were a thing of the past. Teagan was not so sure, but had no way of gauging this apart from the occasional end-of-the-day conversation with the teacher. Teagan was both pleased that he had settled into school, and wary that this may be only a temporary state of affairs. She was eager to support the school in applying for the additional funding and support to which she believed Danny was entitled, but unsure what form that support took in the classroom. She seemed to have been positioned by the school as an interested parent, but also as part of Danny's problem, in that his challenging behaviour was attributed to boredom, particularly at preschool.

Teagan was well aware of her family's role in promoting the educational success of the children. She regarded education as important and wanted her children to achieve positive educational outcomes. For example, she committed a substantial proportion of the family budget to enrolling Danny at preschool, in order to help him experience a positive start to school. While drawing on family stories of education, she used both her and Anthony's non-completion of school as a motivation for her children to achieve something different. Similar findings have been highlighted recently by Turunen (2012). The habitus generated within this family was underpinned by a sense that both parents wanted their children to have opportunities beyond their own.

Conclusion

Families play many important roles in the transition to school, not the least of which involves supporting children as they interact with and among different people, places and contexts over time. Support is expressed and enacted in many ways, including through interactions between parents and children, families and schools, in access to resources and in the generation of supportive home learning environments. The transition to school is a time when families experience changes as those within them adapt to different roles and adjust to different demands. It is also a time of both increased vulnerability and opportunity for families as new relationships and identities are forged and new contexts explored. It is possible to focus on the increased vulnerability and to identify any number of child and/or family and/or community risk factors that may influence engagement with school. As we suggest in this chapter, it is also possible to consider the transition to school as a time of opportunity, aspiration, expectation and entitlement for all involved and to work together to attain the best possible educational outcomes for all children and their families.

Acknowledgements

This research was supported by Australian Research Council Grant LP0669546. We wish to acknowledge the expert assistance of our research colleagues Emma Kearney, Anne Hampshire, Jan Mason and Virginia Schmeid and express our gratitude to the children, families and organisations that participated in the research.

References

Barnes, J., Katz, I., Korbin, J.E. and O'Brien, M. (2006) *Children and Families in Communities: Theory, Research, Policy and Practice*, Chichester, UK: Wiley.

Barton, A.C., Drake, C., Perez, J.G., St Louis, K. and George, M. (2004) 'Ecologies of parental engagement in urban education', *Educational Researcher* 33(4): 3–12.

Bourdieu, P. (1997) 'The forms of capital', in A.H. Halsey, H. Lauder, P. Brown and A.S. Wells (eds.) *Education, Culture, Economy and Society* (pp. 46–58), Oxford: Oxford University Press.

Bronfenbrenner, U. and Morris, P.A. (2006) 'The bioecological model of human development', in R.M. Lerner (ed.) *Theoretical Models of Human Development* (Volume 1 of *Handbook of Child Psychology* (6th edn., pp. 793–828), Hoboken, NJ: Wiley.

Broström, S. (2005) 'Children's perspectives on their childhood experiences', in J. Einarsdottir and J. Wagner (eds.) *Nordic Childhoods and Early Education: Philosophy, Research, Policy and Practice in Denmark, Finland, Iceland, Norway, and Sweden* (pp. 223–256), Greenwich, CT: Information Age.

Dockett, S. and Perry, B. (2007) *Transition to School: Perceptions, Expectations, Experiences*, Sydney: UNSW Press.

Dockett, S. and Perry, B. (2009) 'Readiness for school: A relational construct', *Australasian Journal of Early Childhood* 34(1): 20–26.

Dockett, S., Perry, B., Kearney, E., Hampshire, A., Mason, J. and Schmied, V. (2011) *Facilitating Children's Transition to School from Families with Complex Support Needs*. Online, available at: <http://www.csu.edu.au/__data/assets/pdf_file/0009/154899/Facilitating-Childrens-Trans-School.pdf> (accessed May 2012).

Educational Transitions and Change (ETC) Research Group (2011) *Transition to School: Position Statement*, Albury-Wodonga: Research Institute for Professional Practice, Learning and Education, Charles Sturt University. Online, available at: <www.csu.edu.au/research/ripple/research-groups/etc/> (accessed May 2012).

Einarsdottir, J. (2010) 'Children's experience of the first year of primary school', *European Early Childhood Education Research Journal* 18(2): 163–180.

Griebel, W. and Niesel, R. (2009) 'A developmental psychology perspective in Germany: Co-construction of transitions between family and education systems by the child, parents and pedagogues', *Early Years* 29(1): 59–68.

Hamre, B.K. and Pianta, R.C. (2001) 'Early teacher–child relationships and the trajectory of children's school outcomes through eighth grade', *Child Development* 72(2): 625–638.

Henderson, A.T. and Mapp, K.L. (2002) *A New Wave of Evidence: The Impact of School, Family and Community Connections on Student Achievement*, Austin, TX: National Center for Family and Community Connections with Schools. Online, available at: <http://www.sedl.org/connections/resources/evidence.pdf> (accessed May 2012).

Hoover-Dempsey, K.V., Walker, J.M.T., Sandler, H.M., Whetsel, D., Green, C.L., Wilkins, A.S., et al. (2005) 'Why do parents become involved? Research findings and implications', *Elementary School Journal* 106(2): 105–130.

Langford, J. (2010) 'Families and transitions', in S.L. Kagan and K. Tarrant (eds.) *Transitions for Young Children* (pp. 185–209), Baltimore, MD: Paul H. Brookes.

Nettles, S.M., Caughy, M.O. and O'Campo, P.J. (2008) 'School adjustment in the early grades: Toward an integrated model of neighborhood, parental, and child processes', *Review of Educational Research* 78(1): 3–32.

Peters, S. (2003) '"I didn't expect that I would get tons of friends … More each day": Children's experiences of friendship during the transition to school', *Early Years* 23(1): 45–53.

Siraj-Blatchford, I. (2010) 'Learning in the home and at school: How working class children "succeeed against the odds"', *British Educational Research Journal* 36(3): 463–482.

Turunen, T. (2012) 'Memories of starting school: What is remembered after decades?' *Scandinavian Journal of Educational Research* 56(1): 69–84.

Walker, A.K. and McPhee, D. (2011) 'How home gets to school: Parental control strategies predict children's school readiness', *Early Childhood Research Quarterly* 26: 355–364.

11

RECONCEPTUALISING THE INTER-RELATIONSHIP BETWEEN SOCIAL POLICY AND PRACTICE

Scottish parents' perspectives

Divya Jindal-Snape and Elizabeth F. S. Hannah

This chapter presents the parents' voice regarding their experience of transition practice to provide evidence and make a case for revisiting the links between social policy and practice, and the parents' role in informing them. Survey data were collected from 73 parents in a local authority in Scotland to map early years transition practice onto the recommendations of an Integrated Services Task Group report that informed the content of *The Early Years Framework* in Scotland. We conclude with suggestions for reconceptualising transition policy and practice, and reiterate the importance of parental participation.

The policy context

In Scotland, *The Early Years Framework* (Scottish Government 2008a, 2008b) provides a social policy framework for the development of policy and practice to ensure optimum opportunities for children to maximise their potential. The focus and value placed on the early years, both from individual and societal perspectives, is a distinctive feature of the framework. Children's rights to services that aim to combat potential inequalities, based on race, disability and social background, are encapsulated within the espoused vision. The framework emphasises the key role and contribution of parents, families and communities; the provision of high quality decentralised universal services that place children's needs at the heart of service delivery; and a shift from crisis to early intervention and prevention.

During the development stage of the framework, the Scottish Government established four multi-agency task groups to consider and gather evidence, including commissioned research involving parents and children, and to engage in dialogue with key stakeholders (Scottish Government 2008a, 2008b). The Integrated Services Task Group (Scottish Government 2008c) comprised three sub-groups looking at childcare, preschool and interventions beyond preschool, with the latter considering transitions to school.

As a result of the investigations, the Integrated Services Task Group identified features of effective transition programmes that informed its recommendations for future practice. Through documentary analysis, a number of themes emerged. The recommendations pertinent to the case study in this chapter were closer working partnerships between preschool and primary school staff to ensure continuity of learning for individual children based on sound knowledge of each child's needs; establishing systems for the assessment and identification of children's needs; induction visits for parents and children to familiarise them with the new setting; professionals valuing the role of parents and ensuring they are involved in the transition process; effective involvement and communication with parents; and incorporating active learning approaches in the early years of primary school (Scottish Government 2008c). These recommendations, although not explicitly reported in *The Early Years Framework* (Scottish Government 2008a, 2008b), were influential and explicit reference is made to the work of the task groups and the evidential base.

Researching the transition practice

A case study in one Scottish local authority (LA) explored the links between the six recommendations of the Integrated Services Task Group and transition practice (see Table 11.1). Twelve schools participated in the study and a link to an online questionnaire was made available to parents through the schools. Where requested, paper versions were posted to the schools for distribution. A total of 73 parents, whose children had moved to primary school (Grade P1) six months prior to data collection, responded to the questionnaire. The questionnaire included closed- and open-ended questions that covered their child's and their own transition experience. It was piloted with a group of parents who were not part of the sample.

Sixty-three parents indicated that their child had faced no problems during the transition. A high number of parents indicated that they were happy with the work done by the nurseries ($n = 62$) and schools ($n = 70$) in preparing them and their child for the transition. They highlighted a range of good practice. However, it was clear that practice was not consistent across the early years settings and primary schools in this LA, and that staff and parents could learn from each other. Furthermore, effective aspects of the practice in this LA could inform practice elsewhere in Scotland and overseas. Several themes emerged from parents' responses that map onto the six recommendations (Table 11.1), as explained in the following.

TABLE 11.1 Summary of the fit between Integrated Services Task Group recommendations and parents' views of transition practice in a local authority case study

Recommendations	Parents' perspectives of current practice	Suggestions for improvement
1. Preschool and primary school partnership	• Reciprocal visits • Exchange of information about child • Parents not always aware of the communication	• Involve parents in what and when information is passed
2. Assessment and identification of children's needs	• Evidence of this happening • Focus on maturational approach?	• Better involvement of parents in identifying needs • Strengths should also be identified • Better understanding of secure attachments • Move towards an interactionist approach
3. Induction visits for parents and children; familiarisation	• Children visiting primary schools several months before starting school (up to one year in some cases but a couple of visits in others) • Children joining primary class before the move • Parents visiting schools • In one setting parents visited their children after the move • Induction material • Practice was not consistent	• Good practice should be consistent • Include photos of significant people and places from the school • Use of home artefacts (secure attachments)

TABLE 11.1 (continued)

Recommendations	Parents' perspectives of current practice	Suggestions for improvement
4. Professionals valuing the role and ensuring involvement of parents in the transition process	• Most parents felt involved and valued • Parents able to proactively support their child • Some saw themselves as passive receivers • Some relied on professionals to support transitions and not aware of their own role • Some could not be actively involved in information days due to their work commitment	• Parents should be actively involved and understand the importance of their role in facilitating transition • Flexibility of the programmes may help parents with other commitments to be involved
5. Effective communication with parents	• Seen to be a strength • Lack of feedback about the child settling in	• Opportunities for communication at different points prior to, *and after*, the move to primary school
6. Incorporating active learning approaches in the early years of primary school	• Nurseries preparing children well using active learning approaches • The data are limited in shedding light on the range of active learning approaches in schools	• Further research required

Closer working partnerships between preschool and primary school staff

When asked if parents thought that there was good communication between the early years establishment and the school regarding their child and his/her needs, 56 (76.7 per cent) parents strongly agreed or agreed, 7 (9.6 per cent) strongly disagreed or disagreed, and 10 (13.7 per cent) indicated that they did not know.

According to one parent, an example of good communication between schools and nurseries suggests the new ideas adopted by some organisations:

> Excellent communication between Nursery teachers and school staff. Thought the individual interviews at start of P1 were great idea. P1 teacher knew children before they started.

There is also evidence of good arrangements of reciprocal visits between nursery and school staff and children. However, data also suggest that some parents were not aware of what information was being passed on and when.

Establishing systems for the assessment and identification of children's needs

Although the recommendation on systems for the assessment and identification suggests a focus at the individual child level, it could be argued that it highlights a need to look at systems and structures to facilitate timely and accurate assessment of a child's needs at a critical normative transition point. This was reflected in the experiences of one parent:

> My child was observed by two teachers from the primary school. They felt that her speech was immature and advised a referral to speech therapy! So a meeting was organised on [sic] [an]other chance to assess my child [it] was asked for and I felt it had been handled badly.

And another parent commented on their child's separation anxiety.

Although these were the experiences of two parents, it seems that more work needs to be done in these areas. The importance of secure attachments during periods of transition is increasingly being recognised in policy and practice (Jindal-Snape 2010). *The Early Years Framework* (Scottish Government 2008a) emphasises the importance of relationships and of taking a holistic approach to meeting children's needs. Peters (2010) highlights the importance of children sharing kindergarten portfolios with their primary school teachers and peers. Teachers found these helpful in getting to know the child and his/her strengths (with the focus on *strengths* rather than *needs).*

Familiarisation

School visits for children and parents were seen to be very important in the transition process and 36 parents highlighted them as the most beneficial aspect of the work done by nursery, especially where children were able to join classes and events in the primary school before the move:

> The visits for the children and the parents throughout the year to the primary 1 class to spend time with the teacher and to do some work were very good for the children.

> ... they made a number of trips to the school, e.g. concert, structured play, and the school also ... some P1 pupils to come to nursery play with the children one morning.

This included reciprocal visits from school and nursery teachers:

> Classroom visits and workshops; teachers/head/deputy visits to nursery school; literature sent out to parents.

Moving into school with familiar peers seems to be very important to parents and children. Similar to previous studies (Hannah, Gorton & Jindal-Snape 2010), seven parents said that not moving with friends to the school was a big problem:

> My child was placed in a classroom with children who had previously all been together in a different playgroup, so for the first little while he felt he did not know many of the other children but they [other children] all knew each other.

Further examination of the data showed that 57 (7 per cent) parents indicated that their child had moved into school with friends. However, of the 10 children for whom difficulties with starting school had been reported, 8 children had moved up with friends. Thus not commencing school with a friend appeared not to be related to adjustment difficulties. This is interesting as previous research suggests that children who move with friends find transition to be smoother (Fabian 2000; Margetts 2007). However, given the small sample size of the current study, it is important that nursery/school staff are aware of the importance that parents or children might place on this, and findings also suggest that there are complex issues at play and that getting just one aspect right cannot guarantee a smooth transition.

Professionals valuing the role of parents and ensuring they are involved in the transition process

While parents did not comment about their role being valued by professionals, there is some evidence that parents felt involved in the transition process (see below: Effective communication with parents). Several parents highlighted their role in supporting their children in the transition process:

> As far as I could see my child made the move fairly easily. We visited the school, played in the playground at weekends, and generally put out a 'fun message' that it was a good place to be.

> I feel that I took the time to thoroughly prepare my child for school. The transition was successful and I have a happy wee boy :-)

They also prepared their child for school by making them more independent.

Parents indicated that they followed advice provided in information sent to them by school to prepare their child. However, a couple of parents also expressed that they could have supported their child better if they had information about certain aspects:

> … prepared him for games on the playground if I'd understood what the playground was really going to mean …

However, there is also evidence that some parents saw themselves as passive receivers of information and did not realise that they could play a more active role. Some parents chose not to respond to the question about what they could have done to make the transition experience better and some responded that as the school had done good work they did not need to do much. Not only is the importance of parental involvement in line with the Scottish Government's recommendation, but resilience theory (Luthar 2006) and ecological systems theory (Bronfenbrenner 1979, 1992) also emphasise the importance of focusing on all significant others in the child's environment who play a part in the transition process (Hannah et al. 2010).

Another way in which parents played an important role during transition was by interacting and supporting other parents and children before and after starting school. Several parents indicated that the links with parents of children from their child's school year were helpful. This helped them in organising activities for their children to meet up outside school prior to their child starting school and to get to know other children better:

> … parents have compiled a voluntary list of contact details – helps with arranging out of hours play dates for the children.

There was an indication that most of the communication with other parents once their child had started school was happening every morning and in the afternoon, which becomes difficult for parents who are unable to drop off or pick up their child. One parent suggested that other parents could help by:

> ... top tips on what to expect, i.e the amount of letters from school, special days etc. It was a learning course for me. It took me by surprise just how organised I would have to be ...

In terms of being involved in the transition process, it is interesting that although some parents were using the parent community as a useful resource where they were helping each other, a couple of others did not consider it to be a resource they could tap into. This might suggest that without taking away the autonomy from parents and opportunities to meet at the nursery/school gate or outside the nursery/school, educational establishments could provide opportunities for parents to meet before and after the move within the nurseries and schools. It is also important to emphasise that most parents see it as an opportunity for mutual benefit.

It is important that parents are involved in the transition process. However, it is also imperative to understand that the parents are experiencing transition as well (Jindal-Snape 2010) and might have their own support needs. Sixty-six (90 per cent) parents indicated that they felt that the preparation from the nursery was *helpful to their child*; 5 (7 per cent) disagreed and 2 (3 per cent) indicated that they did not know. However, when asked if the preparation from nursery was *helpful to them*, 63 agreed, 8 disagreed and 2 indicated that they did not know. It is worth noting that there was not always an agreement with satisfaction in terms of the preparation for the child and the parent. Nurseries and schools should be aware of this and provide *consciously planned* support for parents. Further, as one parent implied, there is a need to build relationships between parents and teacher:

> ... I meet a teacher once in a large group and I'm supposed to trust her with my child, why? Because it's socially accepted? This seems weird.

For parents to be effectively involved in their child's transition, it is important that they are supported with their own transition as well.

Effective communication with parents

Parents in this study saw schools' communication with them to be a strength:

> A welcome afternoon, new P1 visited the classroom and received a pack in the post which had information on the school day and a picture to colour and bring along on the day of a character from their first reading

book. The parents had a meeting in the hall where they learned [about] the schools. Policy on many aspects and the P.T.A. gave a chat also.

Data suggest that parents value opportunities to be part of the school and that it is important that they meet all staff rather than the class teacher only:

Communications. Joint meetings for child and separate meetings with parents felt extremely included in the process. Familiarisation visits (several), English and numbers introduction (to familiarise parents to P1 teaching methods).

However, responses also suggest that parents would value more opportunities to speak with the teacher immediately after the child has started school. One parent said:

[school could have] had a parents evening a bit sooner (it was 4 weeks after start of term) or just an informal bit of feedback on how [child was] settling in. Only child's views to go on for first 4 weeks.

Incorporating active learning approaches in the early years of primary school

While the study did not address the types of learning approaches undertaken at school, 55 parents remarked very positively about the preparation from the nurseries in terms of learning and actively undertaking projects related to schools. They highlighted that the main aspects were preparing the child through developing reading/writing skills and independence skills:

Just enough language education given so my daughter wasn't 'lost' when she went to school, but not too much so she was bored in her first few weeks at P1.

The data from the case study suggest a fairly close fit between the recommendations of the Integrated Services Task Group and transition practice. However, there are several areas where further work is required, as can be seen by the parents' and our suggestions for improvement (Table 11.1).

Reconceptualising policy and practice

Similar to previous research (Dockett & Perry 2007), one of the recurring themes in this study was the importance of good and trusting relationships between all stakeholders – pupil and teacher, parents and teacher, child and parents, parents and parents, child and child, nursery and school, and so on. These were developed over time and a conscious effort was required to build these. These link well with the focus on good communication and collaboration of all stakeholders in transition practice as articulated in the Integrated Services Task Group report, and the emphasis on the role of parents and communities in *The Early Years Framework*. It is acknowledged that channels of communication and collaboration processes are complex and have to be consciously built in by different stakeholders.

The role of parents is a key component of contemporary social policy frameworks, such as *The Early Years Framework* (Scottish Government 2008a, 2008b), and legislation, such as the *Scottish Schools (Parental Involvement) Act 2006* (Scottish Government, 2006). Despite such imperatives, it seems that more work needs to be done in terms of improving parental involvement. As we have suggested elsewhere, we need to move towards parental participation, with parents having rights and responsibilities to participate in their child's education (Jindal-Snape, Roberts & Venditozzi 2012). It is understandable that the Framework and Act have put the onus on the professionals; however, it is vital that parents understand the importance of their full participation. In this context we suggest that social policy and practice need to reconceptualise parental participation as being multi-faceted. It is not only about the parents' involvement in the school or their interaction with their child at home; it is also about parents' interaction with each other and providing support during transitions – see the Conceptual Framework of Multi-dimensional Parental Participation (MPP) (Jindal-Snape, Roberts & Venditozzi 2012) for further information.

There is evidence from this study that arrangements were put into place a few months prior to, and after, the move. This suggests that the nurseries and schools were conceptualising transition as a 'one-off event' rather than as an ongoing process, and that the ongoing adaptation needs of the children might not have been considered. However, as the data were limited by being collected at one moment in time and from parents only, it will be important in future research to collect longitudinal data from professionals and children involved in transition.

Policy makers consulting with key stakeholders, as exemplified by the development process for *The Early Years Framework*, is commendable. This should be a model for future social policy development. It is important, however, that research is conducted to establish how policy is informing practice and how the lessons learnt from practice can influence policy. Parents' and children's voice are very important to inform any changes. This should be an iterative process so that research, social policy and practice can inform each other based on ongoing reconceptualisation of the inter-relationship between social policy, professionals and families in the context of transitions.

References

Bronfenbrenner, U. (1979) *The Ecology of Human Development: Experiments by Nature and Design*, Cambridge, MA: Harvard University Press.

Bronfenbrenner, U. (1992) 'Ecological systems theory', in R. Vasta (ed.) *Six Theories of Child Development* (pp. 187–249), London: Jessica Kingsley.

Dockett, S. and Perry, B. (2007) 'The role of school and communities in children's school transition', in R.E. Tremblay, R.G. Barr, R.DeV. Peters and M. Boivin (eds.) *Encyclopedia on Early Childhood Development* (pp. 1–7), Montreal, Quebec: Centre of Excellence for Early Childhood Development. Online, available at: <http://www.child-encyclopedia.com/documents/DockettPerryANGxp.pdf> (accessed 28 May 2012).

Fabian, H. (2000) 'Small steps to starting school', *International Journal of Early Years Education* 8(2): 141–153.

Hannah, E., Gorton, H. and Jindal-Snape, D. (2010) 'Small steps: Perspectives on understanding and supporting children starting school in Scotland', in D. Jindal-Snape (ed.) *Educational Transitions: Moving Stories from around the World* (pp. 51–67), New York: Routledge.

Jindal-Snape, D. (2010) *Educational Transitions: Moving Stories from around the World*, New York: Routledge.

Jindal-Snape, D., Roberts, G. and Venditozzi, D. (2012) 'Parental involvement, participation and home–school partnership: Using the Scottish lens to explore parental participation in the context of transitions', in M. Soininen and T. Merisuo-Storm (eds.) *Home–school Partnership in a Multicultural Society* (pp. 73–101), Finland: Rauma Unit, University of Turku.

Luthar, S.S. (2006) 'Resilience in development: A synthesis of research across five decades', in D. Cicchetti and D.J. Cohen (eds.) *Developmental Psychopathology: Risk, Disorder, and Adaptation* (pp. 739–795), New York: Wiley.

Margetts, K. (2007). 'Preparing children for school – benefits and privileges', *Australian Journal of Early Childhood* 32(2): 43–50.

Peters, S. (2010) 'Shifting the lens: Re-framing the view of learners and learning during the transition from early childhood education to school in New Zealand', in D. Jindal-Snape (ed.) *Educational Transitions: Moving Stories from around the World* (pp. 68–84), New York: Routledge.

Scottish Government (2006) *Scottish Schools (Parental Involvement) Act 2006*. Online, available at: <http://www.opsi.gov.uk/legislation/scotland/acts2006/pdf/asp_20060008_en.pdf> (accessed 13 March 2009).

Scottish Government (2008a) *The Early Years Framework*. Edinburgh: Scottish Government.

Scottish Government (2008b) *The Early Years Framework: Part II*. Edinburgh: Scottish Government.

Scottish Government (2008c) *The Early Years Framework: Final Report from Integrated Services Task Group*. Online, available at: <http://www.scotland.gov.uk/Publications/2008/07/services-report> (accessed 24 June 2010).

PART V

Reframing transition and curriculum

12

CURRICULUM AS A TOOL FOR CHANGE IN TRANSITIONS PRACTICES

Transitions practices as a tool for changing curriculum

Aline-Wendy Dunlop

Transitions research often emphasises the differences children experience as they move from preschool to primary school. The most dominant of these differences are often catalogued as differences in settings, in relationships and in curriculum. A focus has been made on the need to prepare children for school, to support them in their adjustment to school and more recently to advocate the need for schools to change their practices to be 'child ready' so that the changes children need to make to accommodate new experiences are better matched by practices in the new school. Such changes within school may mean a more individualised approach to children and families, and an appreciation of differences between children and parents as well as between systems. The age of transition to school varies across countries and children's capacity to cope with change may develop as they grow older, or in the light of how change has been experienced previously. Where preschools and schools operate together in more tightly coupled systems it is expected that the demands placed on children are more manageable for them. This chapter considers whether curriculum itself can be a tool for change in transitions practices – or perhaps the converse, that transitions are a tool for changing curriculum that has not been serving young children well.

Introduction

Transitions research frequently emphasises the differences children experience as they move from preschool to primary school. Observable differences can often be seen between preschool and school settings, for example in terms of resources, the classroom environment, the emphasis on play-based or paper-based activities, the routines followed and the expectations placed on children. The nature of adult–child relationships also changes during the transition period: parents often raise their expectations of children and day-to-day experiences in school may move along a spectrum of child-centred approaches, negotiated experiences and teacher-centred, teacher-led experiences. Preschool curricula are often more process oriented, whereas school curricula may emphasise knowledge content and skills more (Dunlop et al. 2007).

Children are the link between these systems: it is the children who travel on and so research and practice applications have focused on the need to prepare children to cope with change (Peters 2010), but systems may be able to connect better or differently, allowing us to consider if the continuity between prior-to-school settings and school may be improved.

School entry is a time when 'different contexts, systems, curricula, philosophies and approaches meet' (Educational Transitions and Change (ETC) Research Group 2011: 1). The nature of schooling will determine if school start is likely to be easier or more difficult for school entrants. It has been argued previously that where preschools and schools operate together in more tightly coupled systems it is expected that the demands placed on children are more manageable for them (Fabian & Dunlop 2007). Such demands exist in both socio-emotional and cognitive domains: how change has been experienced previously and whether children are able to respond to discontinuities not only as a challenge (Griebel & Niesel 2009), but also as an opportunity (in itself a definition of socio-emotional competence or resilience), will determine how children navigate school entry and engage in new learning with increasing academic confidence and, arguably, competence.

For the author, therefore, curriculum is a powerful influence on what happens for children in both preschool and school settings and a focus on transitions between these settings is potentially a powerful tool to influence the enactment of curriculum.

Curriculum definition, enactment and experience

Development of frameworks, guidance and curriculum for young children is now commonplace: curriculum has become something that is written down, sometimes conceived of as a process and sometimes viewed through a content lens. There are arguments that curriculum definition has underlined and therefore safeguarded the minimum entitlement of our youngest children to an education. There are counter-arguments that the nature and quality of the curriculum guidance and what it promotes should be critically evaluated.

The systems within which curriculum operates may also determine how curriculum is put into action. Where connections between teachers and settings are strong, then shared working towards improved continuity for children is more likely; where early childhood settings are distinct, geographically separate and very different in approach, then there is less room for negotiation. Where the child's voice is valued, the curriculum is a much more negotiated one and there is more opportunity for children to experience agency (Dunlop 2003a; Reunamo 2007).

The need to interpret curriculum continuity from the child's point of view and experience rather than always from a teacher perspective, to recognise and value children as learners and the ways in which they learn best (Carr 2001; Dweck 1999) and to build on their working theories and 'funds of knowledge', upon who they are, what they bring, how they go about things, are all central to ideas about how curriculum may have an impact on transitions. How practitioners use their knowledge of the child to provide experiences and opportunities is important so that children are given entry points to engage and to display their competence: their funds of knowledge that they bring with them from home or early childhood settings (Peters 2010).

Transitions

Transitions need to be considered not only in a pastoral sense but in terms of children's learning. Such an approach will mean looking at how learning is similarly or differently framed in prior-to-school and school settings, at how the learner is viewed and what the dominant pedagogies are in each setting. While not universal, the enormous shift over recent years in many countries when considering transitions has been twofold – how to bring the worlds of early childhood and formalised schooling closer in terms of their relative familiarity to the child and how to build children's resilience to change. Many contemporary curricula are based on learning outcomes with strong messages about what children should know or be able to do. Too often these targets are blanket age-related criteria that do not take account of individual difference or of adaptive teaching approaches but put faith in taking children through the curriculum without being able to guarantee the learning aimed for. This gap between policy and practice is the central problem of curriculum development (Kelly 2004).

Curriculum based on stage and age theories of development perhaps no longer applies when now conceptions of learning are more focused on sociocultural approaches. But then biology draws me – the young child is in the process of maturing through learning the culture and other forms of meaning-making as language users, storymakers, artists, mathematicians in their daily lives – to the extent that experience and emotional, social and physical prowess allow. The young child is enormously powerful, to be respected, nurtured, followed, allowed to lead and have the chance to show capacity, reveal what they know and invent and to understand what is involved in living alongside others. It is then that contemporary outcomes terminology kicks in – we develop models of what children should know, should learn, should be able to do – and these in educational policy are absolutely determined by age and expectation, so that developmental rather than sociocultural concepts tend to determine early years curriculum.

Who is curriculum for?

Yesterday (any yesterday) I observed two little boys – Archie aged 3½ and his little brother Jack aged 16 months – and I found that age does matter in how we perceive children and whether we are surprised, happy or concerned about how they are doing. Archie has discovered recently that he can draw representationally to intent – a recent birthday card has his family and Grannie and Grandpa surrounding a birthday cake with many candles: lucky Grannie, who I'm sure has The Beatles ringing in her ears, singing 'When I'm 64'! He has also discovered that he can build with lego and has recently started swimming lessons. Observing and listening, I heard Archie's story-making unfold – he built a street of houses and placed a lego person in each, he built a shop with the remaining lego and made sure all the people came one by one from their nearby houses by car, motor bike or 'on their own legs' and returned home. Then I heard him say 'this isn't a shop anymore it's a beach. Everybody is going to the beach, they need to get their clothes off first' – of course lego people have their clothes printed on. His solution was to separate heads and bodies – the heads went off to dive and swim and got dressed (re-assembled) again afterwards. His script took them through conversations, shopping, swimming, putting their washing machines on, reading favourite stories and going to the zoo to see the 'manimals'. He is moving from the systematising of his earlier enveloping schema to a more open imaginative narrative.

Meantime his little brother is cruising the kitchen making announcements about everything he sees, from DOG to MAMA to CAR! – the sounds are much the same but the meaning is clearly defined by expression, place and timing.

These are the people we write curriculum for – do they need it to guarantee their learning or the kind of learning our culture wants to induct them into, or do we write it for adults? Bruner once implied the latter when he said 'A curriculum is more for teachers than it is for pupils. If it cannot change, move, perturb, inform teachers, it will have no effect on those whom they teach. It must first and foremost be a curriculum for teachers' (Bruner 1977: xv). And this is because not all adults engage with children in ways that bring spontaneous learning about, and not all children have the luxury of discovering what they are able to do. Some children do not have the chance to develop funds of knowledge or the communicative and thinking tools to reflect on what they know – and so we talk of getting children ready for learning because some young children have already lost out.

We can also learn from Bruner (1977) not to wait for 'readiness' but to realise with him that children can learn anything at any age if it is presented in 'the child's way of viewing things' at the time. This means building upon what they already know through fostering what Siraj-Blatchford (2010: 86) refers to as 'self-learning and learning to learn'. Central to this in curriculum for transitions is the continuity of experience that can be achieved for children through the transfer of principles between the involved adults, through respecting and fostering children's agency and through collaboration (Bruner 1996).

If indeed curriculum is for the adults who implement it, as suggested by Bruner, then we can see right away how curriculum reform is about changing practices, as well as about the ambitions to change outcomes and to even up the odds – the gaps – that occur in child populations. This is where it is important to consider curriculum as a tool for changing transitions practices.

If policy at preschool/school, local government or national level is aware of the ways in which transitions may affect children, then curriculum enactment provides an opportunity for teachers to recognise what children bring to school, to resist top-down approaches and be more open to combining teacher–planned activity with children's self-directed learning, thus extending children's thinking, moving them on as learners and supporting their changing identity as they become school children.

Transitions practices as a tool for changing curriculum

Research into transitions has shown key differences for children as they make the transition into new educational settings. Children engage in social and emotional interactions in relating to other children, in becoming knowledgeable about the new class or school and in building upon what they already know as they constantly relate to the new. There have been many Scottish initiatives to make transitions smooth for children: the new curriculum offers the potential for transition experiences to focus on continuity within change, rather than on more of the same.

Important factors I have identified in the transition to school in Scotland include teacher collaboration across sectors; parental participation in the transition process; children's agency and voice; and the sharing of information about curriculum and social experiences. Typically preschools and schools arrange visits for new entrants, work hard to build relationships between preschool and school settings, share information about teaching and learning approaches and ensure positive experiences for children and families in the lead-up to school. Patterns of a gradual school start have been replaced in some Local Authorities by a same-day start for all new entrants, but there is an improved awareness of the benefits of cross-sector collaboration, the sharing of knowledge and the importance of creating opportunities for children to build on what they already know, can do and have experienced.

This focus on improved transition experiences has caused reflection on curriculum itself. A transitions working group was set up by Education Scotland to develop transition practices further (Learning and Teaching Scotland 2010). Its report on preschool to primary transitions emphasises the positive impact of the new *Curriculum for Excellence Pre-school into Primary Transitions* (Education Scotland 2010) on such transitions but recognises the continuing need to focus on transitions. It is this focus on transitions practices that will ensure an impact on curriculum and on its implementation. It is essential that children are supported to demonstrate and actively use what they know, and that their skills, their sense of worth and their self-directed learning can bridge into new opportunities constantly and confidently. The glass ceiling of the past – the expectation that all children should be at the same stage in the same class, the view that curriculum is contained and written down – has the potential to shift in a new climate that allows transition experience to influence curriculum and that consequently ensures that curriculum develops in ways that will have an impact on transitions. Bronfenbrenner's (1989) work continues to be helpful here in stressing the inter-relationships between the different contexts or systems that the child occupies – there is a dynamic potential in these system inter-relationships.

In the following three sections the relationships between curriculum and transitions are further explored for their impact upon each other, as shown in Figure 12.1: firstly in terms of how curriculum changes may have an impact upon transitions; then how transitions practices can influence curriculum; and, finally, the benefits of combining approaches to curriculum and transitions in practice.

Curriculum as a tool for changing transitions

Where systems are tightly coupled under the same administrative departments there is a greater likelihood of a shared administrative agenda. Through proximity or intention, preschool providers and schools can develop positive communication around a shared curriculum. Interpretations may vary in how that shared curriculum is implemented, and that is entirely appropriate. The potential to develop shared and mutually understood descriptions of the enactment of curriculum, and how it is experienced by children and teachers, potentially creates a good climate for transition.

This notion of enactment is crucial. A through curriculum for 3- to 6-year-olds may be designed to provide a common, connected and continuous experience, but unless there are shared pedagogical understandings it is unlikely that transitions are much eased for children. Martlew, Stephen and Ellis (2011) explored the use of play-based pedagogy through their study of six Primary 1 classes (the first year of school) in Scotland, in which teachers made moves towards an active play-based approach. They found that children's engagement in class comes from 'active involvement, autonomy and choice' (p. 71): characteristics espoused in preschool education. While this may be accepted practice in prior-to-school settings, it is often challenging for the single teacher in a primary class with larger numbers of children to understand, resource and develop playful learning (Dunlop 2003b). Prior-to-school settings tend to a process-oriented and experiential approach to curriculum experience, while school teachers tend to a content- and outcomes-based approach that Martlew and colleagues describe as teacher-intensive and teacher-initiated approaches.

Impact on transitions ←	1 Curriculum changes ←	3 Combining approaches to curriculum and transitions	2 Transition practices →	Impact on curriculum →
Systems designed to link curriculum potentially provide for curriculum connection and continuity	System curriculum links: – tightly coupled – loosely coupled – no natural linkages		Teacher collaboration and reflection / Visiting between sectors	Teachers working together across sectors to develop continuity and build on prior learning
Process pedagogies going up to school with the child / Content knowledge curriculum drives more formal pedagogy down	Differences in curriculum: – process-oriented curriculum – content-oriented curriculum		Parental participation	Parental interest, support and contribution
Emphasises the importance of shared understandings of young children	An 'active learning' curriculum (a mantra for change, but a definition difficulty)		Children's agency – sharing children's strengths through children's learning stories and various forms of assessment	Children who are able to show their strengths and make use of these in their learning instigate and are active in curriculum – they can make a curricular contribution
Valuing children as learners with existing funds of knowledge	Curriculum that recognises what children bring to school		Transition policy to foster continuity and progression	As sectors work more closely they begin to consider transitions curriculum and learning environments, thus deepening understanding
Risk of age-related silos and general ideas about 'readiness'	Direction of curriculum policy: – age related – top down – bottom up		Shared models of the child	Shared understandings and concepts about young children are helpful in providing appropriately for learning
More attention given to transition challenges and opportunities for children	Policy that focuses on the importance of the early years		Shared pedagogies	Collaboration in appropriate teaching approaches shapes the curriculum offered / Children feel more familiar in similar approaches
Child centredness / Subject centredness / Negotiated curriculum	Differences in curriculum expectations of the child		Continuity in learning	More continuous – new opportunities for learning build positively on the 'known'

Text within column 3 (Combining approaches to curriculum and transitions):

Extending thinking...Moving on as a learner...Creating continuity in change...Cognitive interactions

Working together on relationships, creating connections in environments, views of children

Linking settings ..... Acknowledging curriculum differences ..... Providing for curriculum links

Social/emotional interaction...Forming identity as a school child...Bridging to new opportunities

FIGURE 12.1 The impact of transition practices on curriculum change and the impact of curriculum change on transition practices

Claxton's ideas of intuitive pedagogies (Claxton 2000) are difficult for school teachers, who in letting go of pencil and paper find they struggle to gather the assessment data they rely on to demonstrate effectiveness. So while we might hope to see process pedagogies going to school with the commencing child, the risk is that content knowledge and curriculum definition will drive more formal pedagogy down: a risk that comes from combining preschool and early primary school curriculum. Goouch (2008) suggests that a play-based approach to learning and teaching in school would allow children's drive to learn, their natural curiosities and their search for meaning to continue to flourish.

Thus the Scottish use of 'active learning', although it has been a mantra for change, presents definition difficulties. What in fact does it mean? Is it the same as playful learning or playful pedagogies – is it, as Martlew and colleagues query, about active minds rather than, or as well as, being physically active and playful? While the answers to such questions remain unclear it is essential to continue to interrogate them because, for curriculum changes to have an impact on children's transitions to school, we need to understand the importance of shared understandings of young children and what they bring to learning and indeed to school. The new Scottish curriculum recognises what children bring to school, but do teachers value and build on the concept of children as learners with existing funds of knowledge?

A further tussle is the risk of age-related silos and general ideas about 'readiness'. Children are often judged on their readiness for learning – their 'school readiness'. Such readiness is a generalised concept that includes skills such as writing, or at least recognising your name, managing clothing fastenings and relating to others, rather than focusing on dispositions and learning strengths. When current policy focuses as sharply as it does on the importance of the early years, we can't wait for or nurture 'school readiness' in skills or content knowledge terms, but rather we need to focus on what Trevarthen (2012) has called 'joyful companionship' – learning in the culture and being well-connected with others. The differences in curriculum expectations of the child on entry to school and the shift from child–centred and negotiated pedagogies to what are often more subject-based ones needs to be addressed, for appropriate 'written down' curriculum expectations could have a significant impact on children's transition experiences.

Transitions and curriculum

If, on the other hand, we consider the development of transitions practices, we may want to ask if such practices have an impact on the curriculum experience. This other side of the coin is what I now turn to.

Key elements in effective transition practice include teacher collaboration, parental participation and children's agency. A number of questions flow from these key concepts: how may teachers be supported to collaborate; in what ways can we make space for parental participation; and what is meant by children's agency and how does it help? It is argued here that if these three elements inform transition practices then the curriculum experience of children will indeed change – and improve in relevant ways.

The most important concept here is agency – it underpins professional confidence to act; parents will participate if they feel some agency in the process; and if children feel valued, listened to, respected and have opportunities to make real choices they too will experience agency (Dunlop 2003c; Vandenbroeck & Bouverne De-Bie 2006).

We should not however make the assumption that children necessarily have agency in early childhood settings, nor indeed that children can exert agency at times of transition: sociology has advocated the importance of child participation; the concept of children's voice and the idea of contribution are also important when we consider transitions. Equally, opportunities for parents to participate in their children's educational transitions and to contribute to their 'safe passage' to school give parents agency in this process.

The extent to which educators themselves can exert agency at times of school transitions may be in the hands of the leadership of prior-to-school settings and schools. If, as in the context of the Scottish *Early Level*, collaborating teachers have the gift of curriculum that aims to span the transition to school and to encourage preschool pedagogies reaching into school, they in turn can develop a shared and mutual voice that will foster the sharing of children's strengths through the children's own learning stories and appropriate forms of assessment. In this way children who are able to show their strengths, and make use of these in their learning, instigate and are active in curriculum: they can make a curricular contribution.

If parents, children and educators can work closely together there is the potential to co-construct the transition and to shape curriculum to become a valid transitions curriculum, which considers shared pedagogies, familiar learning environments and a deepening understanding of continuity in learning to build positively on children's existing funds of knowledge.

Agency thus becomes an essential element of transition. Where players have agency, then relationships, settings and curriculum potentially change, and there is an opportunity to see pedagogies changing, environments being considered and the focus of assessment being on the child's contribution rather than on what they can't yet do. It can also be argued that where the players lack agency they simply have to adapt (Reunamo 2007): in that case it is the child who changes, not the system (Dunlop 2004)

Combining approaches to curriculum and transitions

Finally, by making transition connections, settings may be linked in new couplings in which curriculum differences have to be acknowledged and curriculum links made. A combined agentic approach to transitions and to curriculum will create opportunities for them to be mutually influential.

Working together on relationships, creating connections in environments, developing mutual views and respect between practitioners each places a renewed importance on transitions. Where parents and children participate in the process through discussion and planning, this augments the professional contacts and supports continuity in change – one of the prime roles that parents can fulfill in their children's educational transitions (Bohan-Baker & Little 2004).

For practitioners, the expanded thinking that comes through cooperation enhances their efforts to support children to move on as learners, to be focused on the cognitive, social and emotional interaction that contribute to the child's growing identity as a school child and bridges children into new opportunities.

References

Bohan-Baker, M. and Little, P. (2004) *The Transition to Kindergarten: A Review of Current Research and Promising Practices to Inform Families*, Cambridge, MA: Harvard Family Research Project. Online, available at: <http://www.hfrp.org> (accessed November 2012).

Bronfenbrenner, U. (1989) 'Ecological systems theory', in R. Vasta (ed.) (1992) *Six Theories of Child Development: Revised Formulations and Current Issues* (pp. 187–249). London: Jessica Kingsley.

Bruner, J. (1977) *The Process of Education: A Landmark in Educational Theory*, Cambridge, MA: Harvard University Press.

Bruner, J. (1996) *The Culture of Education*, Cambridge, MA: Harvard University Press.

Carr, M. (2001) *Assessment in Early Childhood Settings: Learning Stories*, London: Sage.

Claxton, G. (2000) 'The anatomy of intuition', in T. Atkinson and G. Claxton (eds.) *The Intuitive Practitioner*, Buckingham, UK: Open University Press.

Dunlop, A.W. (2003a) 'Bridging early educational transitions in learning through children's agency', *Transitions, European Early Childhood Education Research Journal*, Themed Monograph Series 1: 67–86.

Dunlop, A.W. (2003b) 'Bridging children's early educational transitions through playful learning'. Keynote presented at a LEGO Research Institute Round Table, *Moving between Kindergarten & School: The Promise of Play*, Staatsinstitut für Frühpädogogik, 11 September 2003.

Dunlop, A.W. (2003c) 'Bridging children's early education transitions through parental agency and inclusion', *Education in the North* 11: 55–65.

Dunlop, A.W. (2004) 'The challenges of early educational transitions: Change the child or change the system?'. *Proceedings of the International Transitions Conference*, University of Western Sydney, November 2003.

Dunlop, A.W., Boyd, B., Skinner, D., Deuchar, R., Mitchell, J. and Smith, I. (2007) 'Literature review of models of curriculum change'. Report for the Scottish Executive Education Department (later Scottish Government) to inform the implementation of 'A Curriculum for Excellence', unpublished.

Dweck, C.S. (1999) *Self-theories: Their Role in Motivation, Personality, and Development*, Philadelphia, PA: Psychology Press.

Education Scotland (2010) *Curriculum for Excellence Pre-school into Primary Transitions*. Online, available at: <http://www.educationscotland.gov.uk/Images/EYTransitions_tcm4-630848.pdf> (accessed June 2012).

Educational Transitions and Change (ETC) Research Group (2011) *Transition to School: Position Statement*, Albury-Wodonga: Research Institute for Professional Practice, Learning and Education, Charles Sturt University.

Fabian, H. and Dunlop, A.W. (2007) *Outcomes of Good Practice in Transition Processes for Children Entering Primary School*, Working Paper 42, The Hague: The Netherlands.

Goouch, K. (2008) 'Understanding playful pedagogies, play narratives and play spaces', *Early Years: An International Journal of Research and Development* 28(1): 93–102.

Griebel, W. and Niesel, R. (2009) 'A developmental psychology perspective in Germany: Co-construction of transitions between family and education system by the child, parents and pedagogues', *Early Years: An International Journal of Research and Development* 29(1): 59–68.

Kelly, V. (2004) *The Curriculum: Theory and Practice* (5th edn.), London: Sage Publications.

Learning and Teaching Scotland (2010) *Curriculum for Excellence Pre-school into Primary Transitions*, Scotland: Transitions Working Group. Online, available at: <http://www.educationscotland.gov.uk/earlyyears/curriculum/transitions.asp> (accessed September 2012).

Martlew, J., Stephen, C. and Ellis, J. (2011) 'Play in the primary school classroom? The experience of teachers supporting children's learning through a new pedagogy', *Early Years: An International Journal of Research and Development* 31(1): 71–83.

Peters, S. (2010) *Literature Review: Transition from Early Childhood Education to School*. Report to the Ministry of Education, Wellington, NZ: Ministry of Education.

Reunamo, J. (2007) 'Adaptation and agency in early childhood education', *European Early Childhood Education Research Journal* 15(3): 365–377.

Siraj-Blatchford, I. (2010) 'Teaching in Early Childhood Centers: Instructional methods and child outcomes', *International Encyclopedia of Education* (3rd edn., pp. 86–89), Elsevier. Online, available at: http://www.sciencedirect.com/science/article/pii/B9780080448947011866> (accessed September 2012).

Trevarthen, C. (2012) 'Growing brains need human companions'. Presentation at the Well Connected Child Seminar, Edinburgh, 7 November 2012.

Vandenbroeck, M. and Bouverne De-Bie, M. (2006) 'Children's agency and educational norms: A tensed negotiation', *Childhood* 13: 127–143.

PART VI
Conclusions

13

BELIEFS, POLICY AND PRACTICE

Challenges

Anna Kienig and Kay Margetts

In this final chapter we bring together the issues that have been presented in preceding chapters and consider implications for reconceptualising beliefs, policy and practice around transition to school. Transitions are an essential part of each child's growing up, particularly in the early years, and the transition to school is part of a lifelong and continuous process, a visible and inevitable marker that children are growing up and their horizons are expanding to meet new people and new challenges (McCormick, Mullins & Townley 2005).

Sociocultural theory provides a framework for understanding how belief systems, cultural values and relationships shape the ways that transition to school and children's development and learning are conceptualised and experienced at the individual and macro-system levels, both directly and indirectly. In this way, starting school is an ecological change in life that is 'both a consequence and an instigator of developmental processes' (Bronfenbrenner 1979: 26). The communication and involvement of all participants is critical in establishing agreed understandings and promoting positive outcomes for all involved (Niesel & Griebel 2005). O'Kane (Chapter 2) contends that transition to school is not only for the individual children and their families, but is also a time of transition to a new educational landscape for all stakeholders in the process, including policy makers.

Reconceptualising beliefs

New approaches and understandings about education provoke new theoretical models, policy development, research and what happens in practice. They invite the re-definition of the role of policy makers, teachers and parents in the education of young children, and of curriculum. The concept of transition to school has moved from it being a static process of developmental change to a more dynamic process and a time of opportunity, aspiration, expectation and entitlement for all involved. It is a time for all involved, at all levels, to work together for the best possible educational outcomes for all children and their families.

Children

We are challenged to reconceptualise how children are included in and how they influence transition decisions and school policy and decisions.

Children have the experience, knowledge and ability to reflect on their experiences of starting school and to identify differences between preschool and primary school. We are reminded of children's agency as they start school and the importance to them of a sense of social, affective and learning competency – the ability to understand and adapt to their new school situation. This includes knowing about relationships and interactions with others, school rules, procedures and ways of doing things, academic skills and taking on a new status and responsibilities (Einarsdottir, Chapter 7; Jensen, Hansen and Broström, Chapter 6; Margetts, Chapter 8). The importance to children of academic skills is foregrounded in the studies of children in Australia and Denmark, and our Danish colleagues report on a play-based approach for supporting literacy development with preschool children.

The perspectives of children reported by Margetts (Chapter 8) demonstrate the close alignments of their ideas about what new children starting school need to know and how schools can help children as they start school, and provide strong evidence for the validity of including children's voices in planning processes. As emphasised by Einarsdottir (Chapter 7), listening to young children not only means hearing but also responding to what children say, and in that way their voices can influence policy and practice. In so doing, we pose a few questions that arise from the children's experiences: How can connections between preschool and school be strengthened to address the sense of disconnection that children report as they move into school? How is learning experienced? What is happening in the playground and how can children's physical and emotional safety and their sense of agency be facilitated? How can relationships be supported and sustained?

Development of future transitions policies have to keep the focus on continuity in children's education and build on their experiences, knowledge and skills so that they experience agency as emphasised by both Einarsdottir (Chapter 7) and Dunlop (Chapter 12). The role of children in this process needs to be reconceptualised and valued in facilitating smooth transitions to school for new entrant children and their families.

Families

Families and communities are important and influential contexts for children as they start school and educational outcomes are supported by cohesive relationships between families and schools. Families provide support for their children at transition, but they also experience a transition themselves and have their own support needs (Dockett and Perry, Chapter 10; Griebel and Niesel, Chapter 9; Jindal-Snape and Hannah, Chapter 11).

Transition to school is a time of increased vulnerability and opportunity for families as new relationships and identities are forged and new contexts explored (Dockett and Perry, Chapter 10), and it is important that parents have opportunities to be agentic: to participate and to support their children's 'safe passage' during this time (Dunlop, Chapter 12). Griebel and Niesel (Chapter 9) have been instrumental in researching the experiences of families, the changes they encounter and the adaptations they make as their children commence school. Parenting is recognised as dynamic and changing, and becoming the parent of a school child as a rite of passage. Changes for parents are associated with their own identities and responsibilities, the loss of relationships as they move away from nursery school and changes to how they integrate the demands of family, school and employment. These are viewed as developmental tasks within the context of parenting. The chance to recognise and deal appropriately with these tasks depends on parents' life circumstances and experiences of schooling. This raises concerns also expressed by Dockett and Perry (Chapter 10) and Petriwskyj (Chapter 4) about how parents of diverse sociocultural backgrounds are supported in this process and the extent to which policy and practice strive to facilitate the inclusion of them and their families.

Families not only support children in the transition process as they interact with and among different people, places and contexts over time, but strong, trusting relationships between all stakeholders – child and teacher, parents and teacher, child and parents, parents and parents, child and child, nursery and school – are also critical. The role of parents is a focus of contemporary social policy frameworks and yet it appears that the rhetoric does not match reality. As Jindal-Snape and Hannah (Chapter 11) stress, there is a need for consciously planned support for parents and for relationship building in the transition process.

The agency of parents in challenging policy in Poland and in advocating for pedagogy that balances their children's socio-emotional and academic learning is empowering and adds credence to the importance of families in educational planning.

By co-constructing transition, both family circumstances and perspectives can be taken into account and the individual and collective habitus of all participants can be valued and respected in the 'schoolification' process (Fabian, Chapter 5; Dunlop, Chapter 12). To do this successfully requires schools to hold positive attitudes, beliefs and perceptions about family engagement and to reconceptualise transition to school as a time of opportunity, aspiration, expectation and entitlement for all involved.

Reconceptualising policy

Research evidence is integral to policy and practice and to sustainable educational practice and outcomes for children. Insight has been provided into the policy context for the early years of school, particularly in Australia, Denmark, Ireland, Poland and Scotland, and some implications for children starting school. We are now seeing transition at the national policy level (e.g. Ireland, Poland, Scotland) and in other countries at the regional or state level (e.g. Australia and Germany), albeit differently. In describing the socio-historical contexts in which changes to policy have occurred, issues are raised that highlight that change at the policy level is complex – sometimes with the interests of children, families and educational institutions at heart, and other times driven or compromised by issues of accountability or fiscal constraints or sometimes both. Many chapters highlight the impact of change at the macro-system level on other levels of society, and vice versa. This is illustrated by the situation in Poland, in which controversies among parents, teachers and educational authorities over changes to the school entry age and the resulting public protest by parents have delayed the implementation of the changes – reinforcing the importance of wide consultation and cooperation between all stakeholders in the development and implementation of policy, and emphasising that change takes time.

The focus on early childhood is in many ways driven by socio-political beliefs and is a tool by which governments invest in their economic futures. It is imperative that the focus by governments on academic outcomes and international competition for high ratings in international test regimes such as PISA and TIMMS does not diminish the importance of children's socio-emotional, physical and spiritual well-being in the early years of schooling, particularly in our rapidly changing world in which adaptability and resilience are increasingly important. In Chapter 6, Jensen, Hansen and Broström note that the implementation of national tests in Denmark has brought about unintended pedagogical practice in day care services, with some pedagogues prioritising academic learning at the expense of crucial care elements. Policy initiatives of educational inclusion in Australia, while aiming to recognise and support the diversity of learners, outcomes for children and transition to school, have been criticised for emphasising readiness and normative development over inclusive provision for diversity. These are salutary warnings that, in seeking to promote lifelong learning, governments must be careful to look beyond the easily measured academic outcomes and value intersubjectivity and lived situations, the mastering of objects and social phenomena. The importance of social, emotional and communication competence is reiterated by Kienig (Chapter 3), Fabian (Chapter 5) and Dunlop (Chapter 12), and also by the children in the studies reported by Einarsdottir (Chapter 7) and Margetts (Chapter 8). More is needed to bring greater understanding and valuing of these competencies between sectors of the educational community at large. Aline-Wendy Dunlop

(Chapter 12) stresses that this is more likely to occur when sectors or systems are coupled under the same administration departments, but we do need to be mindful that while transition to school is a universal passage, the substance is cultural: one model does not fit all.

In addressing transition to school, attention to longer-term strategies, clearer policy settings and systemic educational change is needed; relationships with families and communities and profession learning in teachers are needed (Petriwskyj, Chapter 4).

Reconceptualising practice

Associated with reconceptualising beliefs and policy we have also reconceptualised some aspects of practice and the relationship to curriculum. However, attention to further implications for practice from our work is needed and here the diagram developed by Dunlop (Chapter 12, Figure 12.1) is a useful tool.

The ways that early childhood education and care, the early years of schooling and transition to school have been constructed vary from country to country. For some, the external force of policy is placing strenuous demands on the organisational context at the preschool and school level and also on pedagogy. Policy changes must be supported by pedagogic changes (Petriwskyj, Chapter 4; Dunlop, Chapter 12). In addressing the unexpected conflicting demand of academic leaning over the socio-emotional pedagogic tradition, Jensen, Hansen and Broström (Chapter 6) propose an approach to language acquisition and early literacy in preschool and the early years of schooling where communicative competences are seen as interwoven with dimensions of empathy, the social settings and an overall pedagogical sensitivity towards the child as a maker of meaning. Supporting the notion of greater coherence between the pedagogies of preschool and school, Petriwskyj (Chapter 4) raises awareness of the importance of increasing teacher awareness of the theories underpinning transition and their practice, including professional learning for teachers in cultural diversity and sustained specialist educational support for children with disabilities and those who experience educational disadvantage. The question is, to what extent do teacher education courses specifically address transition theories, policy and practice? It is important that the prevailing view of sociocultural diversity as a deficit is reconceptualised to enhance inclusion and transition.

On reflection

There are still gaps in our understanding of transition, and further research and reconceptualisation are needed. While the rhetoric emphasises the importance of co-constructed transition, the evidence suggests otherwise – and the 'silences' need to be addressed. As illustrated by O'Kane (Chapter 2), where gaps are identified and research around them follows, then policy and practice are better informed.

We need to know more about policy at the school level: To what extent do schools have policies and tangible guidelines for transition in place to which they are accountable, or do they have a vague collection of strategies and activities? To what extent are policies and practices inclusive of all members of the community? Whatever is in place, they should be reviewed regularly to keep them up to date and owned by all those involved.

We need to know more about what is happening at the prior-to-school level: How do educators and pedagogues perceive starting school and how do they support children during transition? To what extent do schools proactively make connections with prior-to-school services and families? To what extent have recent policy changes impacted the curriculum and pedagogy? To what extent does transition inform curriculum?

With an increasing recognition that personal well-being empowers children as learners (and we would argue that it also empowers parents), issues of social exclusion, marginalisation and dissonance have been raised; and yet there is reportedly limited research and effective practice currently around these important issues, particularly for minority ethnic groups and for families disconnected from educational opportunities by distance, illness or disability.

In concluding, there is much to challenge us as we move forward in our understanding of just how complex transition to school is, and seek to reconceptualise existing policy and practice within a sociocultural framework in which we better understand the importance of joint participation, communication and the sharing of information within and between systems for more sustainable educational policy and practice.

Saliently, Fabian (Chapter 5) reminds us: the transition process cannot be hurried.

References

Bronfenbrenner, U. (1979) *The Ecology of Human Development: Experiments by Nature and Design*, Cambridge, MA: Harvard University Press.

McCormick, K., Mullins, B. and Townley, K. (2005) *Transition in Early Childhood*, Frankfort, KY: Kentucky Department of Education.

Niesel, R. and Griebel, W. (2005) 'Transition competence and resiliency in educational institutions', *International Journal of Transitions in Childhood* 1: 4–11.

INDEX